MENTAL EXERCISE FOR

Dogs

The Best Dog Games for Improving Behaviour, Strengthening
the Bond, and Having Fun Together - Benefits for
Both You and Your Furry Friend

CHARLOTTE NELSON

TABLE OF CONTENTS

INTRODUCTION

MENTAL EXERCISE FOR DOGS

CHARLOTTE NELSON

E very meal you make, every treat you bake, every bite you take, every chew you make, I'll be watching you.

Does that sound like a certain someone, you know, very hairy and with four legs?

Oh wow! You either bought one or already have one, but regardless, this hairy creature is standing in front of you, and you have fed, tickled, and cooed over the critter, but that doesn't seem to be enough. Besides, unlike Barbie or any other toy, this hairy breath of doggo did not come with any instructions—and certainly wasn't neatly packaged with a "Made in Mattel" stamp accompanied by a warranty. What to do now?

There's no point in crying like a wolf now; you're part of the pack, so you might as well get used to it.

Ready to roll with it?

Yes, indeed you are! And you are going to have to dive right in and start understanding "dog". Think positively now, because at least it's not some biology exam in a foreign language with handwriting that looks like an onslaught of scribbles and pronunciation that consists of five consonants after each other. Well, it might seem as such at first, hence let me redeem myself and say at least there is no grammar.

You have a real pet, not a pet rock. This critter is breathing, living, and experiencing emotion. And you know what else? This is probably one of the best things that has ever happened to you, because what is contained within those little hairy bodies is nothing but love and joy. It is your responsibility to unlock that and fully experience it.

This is most likely one of the best investments you will ever make. Who says money can't buy love? Perhaps in some instances adopt love? Yes, you can—in both instances—when it comes to four-footers. For a few treats and possibly a little more, such as time and attention, but the fact remains that having a hairy, furry, four-footed, trusty companion is worth every bit of effort you put in to strengthen that character and develop one of the best bonds you will ever have.

Let's kick off by talking about relationships. What would you say are some of the first key elements that springs to mind?

Maybe good communication, mental stimulation, quality time, and an awareness of each other's needs? And it is no different when it comes to your doggo—perhaps you are privileged enough to have more than one. Irrespective of how many fur balls you are surrounded by, these are solid principles that form the foundation of any healthy, long lasting relationship that benefits both, or all, parties involved.

But what's the difference here between human and doggo relationships?

In truth, and as you will see with further reading, not much. Dog-human relationships, like human-human relationships, can influence each other on multiple levels, including behavioral responses, welfare, and physiological aspects. As a result, the most important thing to remember as a pet owner is that no critter is beneath you. Yes, they cannot go out and start a business, rent a house, or purchase medical insurance, but their emotional experiences are very much similar to ours.

And where does this leave you as a doggo parent?

In short, pretty much with the ball in your court!

You are the one with cognitive awareness, a sense of responsibility, and the alpha in dog-human relationships. The king of the roost, the pack leader, the cream of the crop. This all sounds great, and having those accolades is wonderful, but how do you provide *value*?

This is not a simple answer, hence I wrote this book to provide you with a springboard that could catapult you into earning your stripes as a dog parent. And the most beautiful news ever is the fact that transforming a doggo's life to a more obedient, self-controlled one would mean that you have the same as well. After all, you are most probably partners in crime, having each other's backs, and there is nothing wrong with that. But the one golden rule with regards to any friendship, and that is that all parties involved must have a positive influence on each other. If not, it would be deemed as a toxic relationship. One party gives and another party takes. And this is not at all what healthy relationships are about, they are about equally giving and receiving.

We are all so focused on the physical, especially in this modern world where everything has to appear perfect, that we frequently, if not most of the time, overlook the root of our well-being—specifically the mental aspect. This is especially true with regard to pets. They are not just an accessory to make a person look or feel good; they, too, have their hearts broken, misgivings of depression, and low self-esteem, among other things. Thus, better understanding how to provide for them, not just physically, but also mentally, is critical.

Don't go overboard and work yourself up into an Italian love knot right now; it's all based on knowledge and understanding. Yes, you're probably thinking, another textbook lecture. You might be surprised; it's short and sweet, and you'll put this book down and look at your cuddly fur ball with a lot more confidence.

Trying something new in life can be frightening for most of us because we are creatures of habit, and no one would dare to change that fact over there. Growth, on the other hand, necessitates change, and with doggo, change is something to look forward to. Because beneath that furry, pink-tongued, wagging-tailed, four-footed fuzzball is a wealth of talent, extra personality, independence, and happiness waiting to be released. Even better, you could be a part of it; seeing joy, happiness, and fulfillment light up in your fido's beady eyes would fill your heart with contentment and a sense of purpose, regardless of the fact that you can trust them with your house and heart, but never with your sandwich.

Before we all get a dog short of crazy, I would just love to, very briefly, scan through what you might expect, without it being a spoiler alert.

We will look at various topics such as the importance of physical and mental stimulation, what to do and what to avoid, some suggestions and solutions, exercises, and finally mental health awareness.

Enough with the questions; let us now move on to finding solutions to all these questions and discovering how you can have fun while teaching that beloved pooch of yours.

CHAPTER 1:
THE IMPORTANCE OF BUSY BODIES

MENTAL EXERCISE FOR DOGS

CHARLOTTE NELSON

You will be pleasantly pleased to learn how important physical activity and regular exercise is for your cuddly canine's physical and physiological well-being.

Why is this the case?

In simple terms, this is because the advantages are similar to the ones you get from engaging in regular physical exercise. As a result, it is quite acceptable to infer that, just as you should not ignore these elements of yourself, your devoted friend should not be disregarded.

As with you, it is never too late to adopt a well-thought-out fitness regimen for your wonderful mongrel—regardless of age, size, or breed. Regular exercise improves conduct, attention, comprehension, and calmness. And the best part about this is that it will keep you going and further gaining benefits from it as well. Almost like getting two things for the price of one!

Aside from keeping them limber and agile, it is an excellent approach to help them better manage their anxiety-related behaviors, which may include chewing, excessive barking, digging, or licking. Emotionally, you will be building and sustaining trust, which is a critical component of every healthy, successful relationship. After all, providing you with such camaraderie and spending some time out of your schedule to ensure their tiny hearts are beaming is not much to ask.

As they say, the devil is in the details, so let us proceed and focus on the physical and psychological benefits that your lord or lady of the manor may enjoy.

PHYSICAL BENEFITS

Forget the notion that you are merely their persistent personal scratcher, because making sure they keep active is a sure-fire method to improve their lifespan. Which means you can gaze into those beady little eyes for a lot longer.

Let's look at the physical advantages regular physical exercise will bring:

Prevents Premature Aging

You are probably having a good chuckle at this one, but it's not all about looks. Age-related physiological changes in our dogs' muscle mass increase their vulnerability to illness and disease risks as well as slower recovery times. This is countered by muscle integrity and strength, which, you guessed it, are achieved by regular exercise.

Regulates Weight

Given that obesity is one of the main health issues affecting dogs in particular, it is even more imperative to keep them moving so that their weight can be regulated and their metabolism can be addressed. They run the risk of contracting various ailments due to obesity, such as bone disease, cancer, chronic inflammation, and even depression, to mention a few.

Joint Health

Your four-legged follower's joint health is a top priority. Regular exercise alleviates joint pain, increases joint lubrication, and strengthens surrounding muscles—allowing joints to be appropriately supported.

Helps with Arthritis

Arthritis is yet another harsh truth that stares your strolling buddy in the face, and a sedentary lifestyle has the potential to exacerbate this painful disease. Regular exercise not only helps relieve arthritic pain, but it also decreases the body's inflammatory potential by reducing adipose tissue storage, which is loose connective tissue that stores fat.

Eliminates Toxins

When doggo is out and about exercising, his working muscles facilitate his lymphatic system pumping toxins and metabolic by-products out of the body. And just as great as you tend to feel after a workout due to the release of toxins and stress, so does your trusty companion.

Improves Insulin Health

Insulin resistance and diabetes are also causes for concern in your furry friend. Regular physical exercise helps the gene system regulate insulin in their bodies, improving biological age, energy, strength, and stamina.

Improves Cardiovascular Health

Doggo's blood pressure and heart health will all improve, leaving them less susceptible to heart disease with a consistent cardio activity that includes activities such as jumping and running for instance.

Healthy Digestion

Nutrient absorption and improved gastrointestinal health are two other benefits that you can expect through regular physical activity, which contributes to healthy digestion.

MENTAL BENEFITS

Dogs laugh with their tails, and what goes on in their little heads should not be disregarded; they also experience joy and suffering, and, like us, can acquire mental health illnesses such as depression.

People are sometimes overly concerned with their cuddly pet's physical health, and the cerebral side of things tends to get overlooked. However, as your companion ages, he or she requires a lot more mental stimulation than younger critters. Because they cannot be entertained socially or go for walks, mental stimulation is especially important for your doggo if he or she has any physical limitations as well.

Let us look at the impacts physical activity has on your beloved companion's mental health.

Improved Mood

A happy hound is a cognitively stimulated hound, and frequent physical exercise increases brain activity, which keeps depression and stress at bay. This reduces boredom, which improves behavior since they are calmer. Before you know it, bad habits such as clawing in the trash or ripping up your couch for instance, will be a thing of the past.

Reduces Hyperactivity

Games, learning new tricks, and walks are all excellent methods to keep that pickle poked while boosting concentration and burning stamina. This helps them to release a lot of pent-up energy and redirect it into more useful pursuits.

Aids Against Cognitive Decline

Cognitive decline is still another issue to keep an eye on. Just as your memory may become hazy as the years go by, so may your pet's. Keeping that mind engaged is a fantastic way to keep those neural connections firing and wiring, helping keep cognitive decline at bay.

Forges Your Bond

Team work is what makes the dream work, and similarly, spending time with your canine companion strengthens your relationship so that you two start to resemble two peas in a pod. This will greatly reduce the likelihood of disobedient conduct.

Encourages Good Behavior

Physical activity, especially for puppies, is fantastic for not only releasing some of the excess energy they have in their small bodies, but also for improving their confidence via socialization from a young age—all of which contributes to greater future mental health.

Reduces Anxiety

Regular physical exercise helps keep anxiety at bay and, again, reduces negative attention seeking behaviors such as excessive chewing or digging up the backyard.

Fights Against Depression

Depression may wreak havoc on your dear pal's mental health. This might be caused by a change in environment, neglect, or even loss. Basically, anything that may send you into a depression spiral could also have an impact on your canine partner. Thus, the fact that they have four legs and are slightly more hairy than a human companion should make no difference when it comes to connecting, expressing compassion, and ensuring that they are cognitively and physically occupied. As regular physical exercise is beneficial to human mental health, it is also beneficial to your pet's mental health, so that daily stroll does more than simply keep the muscles limber; it also promotes a happy hound with a sound mind.

Due to a lack of physical activity and mental stimulation, all the factors we have discussed that are advantageous to your companion could be adversely impacted. This could result in a number of health problems, including obesity, anxiety, depression, joint problems, and even muscle atrophy.

The amount of mental and physical stimulation required by your pet varies according to breed. Dogs such as Jack Russells, huskies, shepherds, boxers, and pointers require more excitement than other breeds. Check in on your breed and the amount of stimulation they require to strike that perfect equilibrium.

A healthy 20 minutes of cerebral stimulation every day would suffice on average. Physical activity is again determined by breed and age. A puppy would require greater physical exercise because of their high energy levels, but this should be done in short bursts throughout the day as their bodies are still developing. It all depends on the breed and level of health with regards to older critters. If your dog has any physical problems or limitations, it is recommended that you consult with your veterinarian before engaging in any physical exercise to ensure that your pet is on the safest, most effective regimen.

On the other hand, your pet may get overstimulated, leading them to feel overwhelmed and display behaviors like hiding, excessive panting, pacing, or barking. This is known as hyper-arousal, and it is caused by either too much positive or negative stimuli. If you detect any of these indicators, remove your companion from the situation and enable them to take some time out in a peaceful environment to help them relax.

The greatest thing you can do is monitor and evaluate how much exercise your wonderful mutt requires; after all, you know them best.

Let's go on and look at some interesting facts that will help you better read and comprehend their behavior, essentially becoming more fluent in "dog".

CHAPTER 2:
CANINE
COMMUNICATION

Your fluff ball does talk, but you must learn to listen; they communicate mostly through body language. Thus, do not think because they fall short of a vocabulary that could put Merriam Webster to shame they are not talking, participating, or comprehending you.

Surely you can identify with a few unusual occasions where you were staring at that four-legged gem of yours, voicing an insight and receiving a wordless stare that indicates "Wow, I never thought about that".

Alas, let us go into the realm of canine communication, which will help you better evaluate what your faithful companion may require and also allow you to strengthen that bond.

INDICATORS

You should look all over that hairy body, scanning every inch, because no one signal or bodily part of your magnificent mutt functions independently. It is a presentation that you should understand; fortunately, it is not rocket science. Let's start with some cues that you need to be aware of.

Wagging Tail

Ladies and gentlemen, we have the loose wag, the low-hung, and the high-stiff, and these are not cocktails, rather, they are dog tails.

A wagging tail is in fact more than simply a tale of joy. Dogs' tails are wagging and waving about at various speeds and elevations, communicating varied messages to you. When that rhythm starts up, you should be aware that the degree of excitement increases as well, but be cautious because excitement and aggressiveness exert and manifest in the same ways at times when that burst of energy requires to be released, hence biting, mouthing, or leaping is to be expected.

- The Loose Wag

  Usually swinging in a steady circular motion at mid-height, the loose wag is, as the name implies, loose and tranquil in a neutral position. This is suggestive of a pleasant, calm companion.

- The Low-Hung

  Uncertainty or anxiety is generally indicated by low-hung tails, regardless of how briskly the air is stirred. Thus if that tail is unusually low, take it as a sign that your care bear is a scared bear.

- The High-Stiff

  That raised, stiff tail can signify agitation, anxiousness, and submissiveness when they are scared, which could make them act aggressively to fend against the fear they are experiencing.

A fascinating truth is that the direction in which your dog's tail wags can also indicate whether or not they are happy. A study found that when their wags are to the right, it is a good indicator that they are pleased and experiencing positive emotions, and when they are to the left, it is related with unpleasant sensations. Finally, they are definitely delighted when they become so animated that they appear to be akin to a helicopter about to take off doing the all-too-familiar helicopter tail wag (Quaranta et al. 2007).

Barks

Don't be tricked into thinking that your dog's barks are similar to your vocals; they do utilize it to help get certain messages across, but focusing on their body language is far more telling of their emotions.

This is not to say you should ignore such barks; you will notice distinct tones and intensities, for example, when they are excited versus alert, or perhaps those barks that have the magical capacity to nibble away at your conscience when they want to get inside the house.

Ear Position

Now, it is very easy to gauge their moods by looking at those ears, however, depending on the ears, since sharp, pointy ears are much easier to figure out than others.

Let's take a quick look at some signs that can be detected even with a pair of Dumbo auricles, as basset hounds have.

- Backwards

    When the ears are pulled backwards your companion is feeling insecure, unsure, nervous and scared.

- Forwards

    This indicates that they are on high alert, whether because they are curious or disturbed. It's best to narrow down which one by observing other body language cues.

- Relaxed

    When their ears are relaxed, maybe drooping to the sides, this signifies they are comfy and content.

Facial Expressions

Even though it might be perplexing at times when it comes to dogs, this is likely going to be the best news ever, they can actually smile!

The strange thing is that it may be rather frightening at times, yet it is not accompanied with the sound effects of an angry gnarl. But again, rely on other body language cues to discern if you are being charmed or confined to the dog box when those frontal smile bones are exposed.

Their facial emotions are very much comparable to that of us humans, as they lick their lips while savoring something good, but also when they are feeling anxious. They also yawn, signifying boredom, or fatigue. They may, however, produce a yawn when they are agitated and stressed; yawning aids in calming them down.

All in the Eyes

Yes, you guessed it: they are also the windows to the soul when it comes to your faithful companion's eyes, because peering into those beady tiny spheres may reveal a lot.

Eyes that are comfortable, almost seeming as if you just want to slip a pair of sunnies on them, all smooth and relaxed, denotes satisfaction. Cold, hard stare eyes indicate hostility, especially when they are staring at something for prolonged periods of time. They also glance away or avoid eye contact when they are distressed; this is not your companion ignoring you, but rather a sign of discomfort.

Whale eyes, which is when there is a lot of the white part exposed, serves as an indication of discomfort as they may be apprehensive or agitated.

Perfect Posture

When it comes to your caring canine, weight distribution speaks louder than words, and these are typically extremely easy to judge because they have a tendency to be highly animated in nature.

For example, if your four-legged companion hunches and lies low to the ground, making their postures smaller, this is an indication of stress, almost as if they are surrendering and intend no harm. They can even expose those bellies, which you could mistake for wanting a good old belly scratch, but when it is frequently accompanied by some urinating, it could be a sign of discomfort and vulnerability. Then there's the adorable play bow gesture, in which the chest is lowered to the ground and the rear reaches for the stars, signaling playfulness and excitement.

We all wish to seem taller at times, and when it comes to your companion, standing tall and shifting body weight forward may indicate interest. This attitude, along with a high tail, may suggest that your mutt is on the defensive, hence trying to appear taller and more intimidating. Finally, the paw raise is rather common in some breeds because it is how they gesture towards prey, but if your companion does not fall into this classification, a paw raise or pointed paw is an indication of insecurity and some tender love and care is required.

CUES

Can you imagine what it would be like if you could fully comprehend what your perfect pooch is saying? They deserve to be heard.

Let's look at some signals now that you are more aware of the indicators to look out for.

Fear Cues

These signs are displayed when your buddy is upset, scared, or uncomfortable.

You'll have to retain your cool a lot of the time because there may be other indicators involved when your companion seeks to self-soothe throughout these instances. There is just one answer when it comes to this, and that is to remove your furry friend from the circumstance that is causing them distress.

Look for the following indicators:

- whale eyes

- tucked tail, usually between the legs

- lifted front leg

- displaying teeth

- weight is shifted towards the back with regards to posture

- facial tension and tight lips

- leaning away

- flattened ears

- sweaty paws

- exposing the belly

- raised hackles, when the fur rises along the back

- pacing, howling, growling, whining, or snarling

- excessive drooling and dilated pupils

- excessive shedding and dandruff

- frozen mobility

Calm Cues

Doggo uses calming signals for a variety of reasons, all of which are depending on the context of the scenario—giving you a better understanding of the next moves you should take.

These signals are used by your magnificent mutt to self-soothe when they are:

- feeling stressed
- overly excited
- in need of a break

The following indicators are tell-tale signs:

- stretching
- licking lips
- yawning
- panting
- sniffing
- scratching
- sighing

Whether they are worried, too thrilled, or in need of a break, they will need to be calmed down and comforted; nevertheless, once again, the best thing to do is to remove your buddy from the situation. If they simply required a short break from playing, a momentary time out to allow them to recuperate would do just fine.

Relaxed Cues

When this is a signal, you should know they are in a happy place, perfectly content with life as it is. Of course an additional scratch or cuddle would always be welcome.

- relaxed tail
- open mouth
- squinty, soft eyes

Play Cues

When any of these indicators arise, you have an eager beaver, ready to have fun and the game is on, so be sure to have plenty of energy in addition to the toys you'll need to pull out all the stops.

Some indicators include the following:

- the infamous play bow
- loose, wiggly movements
- bouncing
- rapid movement with interludes of brief pauses

Alert Cues

Alertness may include indications of being distressed or excited. Therefore a level head is required yet again, taking the context into account, as well as fine tuning into all aspects of body language. However, proceed with caution if you detect alert cues.

Keep an eye out for the following:

- pitched ears

- ears leaning forwards

- stiff, high tail

- tense, closed mouth

- frozen stance

- forward lean in posture

Lack of effective communication in most relationships is one of the greatest issues after all, isn't it?

But now you can confidently assert that, when it comes to your cherished friend, you can talk the talk and walk the walk. A better understanding of your doggo allows for a better bond to form. This makes you a better companion, leader, and teacher by enabling you to be more successful in attending to your partner's needs. Money can buy you a lot of things, including any dog you desire, but only love and understanding can make him wag his tail and become one of the finest companions you will ever have.

Now comes the exciting part: toys! We all have a child within us, regardless of how many years we have on the clock, and this also rings true when it comes to your furry friend.

CHAPTER 3:
TOYS

MENTAL EXERCISE FOR DOGS

CHARLOTTE NELSON

You wouldn't leave a human, adult or kid, at home without food or other types of stimulation, and the same is true for your friendly fido.

Remember, if you have to leave the house for work, the shops, or any other reason and your dog needs to stay at home, you must provide some form of stimulation to keep that sofa or pricey pair of shoes from becoming the next great chew toys. Stocking up on dog toys is one of the simplest methods to keep your companion busy, keeping their small hearts and minds from falling into despair as a result of missing you too much.

Not just any dog toys will do; the greatest alternative for protecting your shoes and furnishings is to choose cognitively challenging toys, keeping boredom at bay.

Let's take a look at some of the variables you should consider while purchasing toys.

CONSIDERATIONS

Variety is wonderful, but when it comes to getting your snuggle bear the ideal toys to keep them amused and engage their intellect, it might be a little perplexing. So, before dipping into your pockets, let's have a look at some fundamental factors you should consider.

Variety

Yes, you enjoy variety, as does your lord or lady of the manor. Regardless of how possessive they are about their toys, you must step in and keep the show going by rotating their toys, presenting them with fresh alternatives, and therefore consistently stimulating them. Thus, even if your doggo is crazy about balls, there's no harm in having a small collection going. To keep that peanut ticking, you should spice things up by introducing different types of toys. This would prevent them from taking creativity into their own paws and honing in on your home's furniture.

Size

They say size does matter, and indeed it does when it comes to functionality and safety with your doggo. It's about finding that perfect balance, not too small in order to avoid choking and not too big in order for them to still be able to drag and carry it around. Be sure that you know your dog's mouth size as well as you know your own shoe size when it comes to making toy purchases.

Age

Age is more than just a number, because it is often strongly related to our energy levels. This stands true whether you have two legs or four legs. In general, between the ages of ten weeks and one year, you may expect bursts of energy and elevated amounts of playfulness from your canine; nevertheless, do not neglect the essential teething period. During this stage, pups will want chewable toys as well as toys that help them expend their energy.

More cognitively stimulating choices would be ideal for older mutts.

Personality

You wouldn't purchase a youngster a toy car if they are into barbies, likewise with your doggo. Canines consist of different characteristics that all constitute each of their own distinct little personalities. Some may be shy, while others may be boisterous; thus, before purchasing a basic soft toy for your energetic friend, consider whether they would be happier with a chew toy for instance. A more reserved personality would not love a squeaky toy and may prefer soft toy selections instead.

These are just a few pointers to expand on that canine toy-time knowledge of yours, let's move forth and look at some toys.

Hygiene

Your dog's toys would need to be cleaned on a regular basis to remove all of the filth, grime, and drool, as well as to keep bacteria and other pathogens at bay that collect from all of the clobber, chewing, and loving these items undergo.

TOY TYPES

It is simpler to determine what toys to buy if you have a deeper understanding of that significant character. Thank goodness there are a plethora of options available to appeal to the huge range of furry personas out there.

Let's have a look at some of the interactive dog toys on the market that are sure to keep your pal intellectually engaged. However, they are merely guidelines to give you something to gauge by. There will be numerous similar solutions available on the market. At the end of the day it is all about what suits you and doggo best and, as long as that furball can play fetch and have his fancy tickled, all is good.

Here are a few of the most noticeable discoveries:

All of the products mentioned are available on Amazon.com (Amazon, 2022).

Balls

What a delight it is to see your doggo get such a great deal of pleasure from something so basic, a ball? Balls are pretty standard when it comes to the majority of mutts' toy collections, this basic object is ideal for playing fetch and doubles up as a chew toy as well. I mean, tossing it into water for those doggos who believe they have the magical ability to transform into a hairy mermaid and go grab it out of the water is just too much fun. Furthermore, there is nothing more loving than a wet dog, they say. But it doesn't matter, water or land, just make sure you have the appropriate size to avoid choking.

☐ The *Outward Hound Nina Ottosson Treat Tumble* is a ball that is a lovely option for a treat-dispensing puzzle toy. They sniff the treats and keep rolling the ball around in order to release them.

☐ With its sound effects and bouncy rubber feel, the *ChuckIt! Ultra Squeaker Ball* comes in a range of sizes and is ideal for fetch.

☐ The *Gnawsome Medium Squeaker Ball* has a soft spiky texture that is perfect for massaging the gums, as well as an inbuilt squeaker to keep them interested. These come in a variety of sizes as well.

☐ The *Franklin Pet Supply Squeaky Dog Tennis Balls* are essentially tennis balls with sound effects.

☐ A DIY alternative: A good old tennis ball will do just fine.

Rope Toys

These are composed of rope, as the name says, and are ideal for playing fetch or tug of war. Another fascinating feature about rope toys is that they may help keep your dog's teeth clean by serving as floss when they tug and bite down on it, eliminating food and massaging their gums.

☐ The *Mammoth Flossy Chews Color Rope Tug Toy* is a knotted piece of rope made of non-toxic Cotton-Poly yarn that is ideal for tug or retrieve.

☐ The *SPOT Colorful Rope Bungee Dog Toy* is yet another rope toy variation, and believe me, there is a wide range of rope toys available. Ones that are looped and knotted and are attached with balls, bottles, or plushies of various colors.

☐ A DIY alternative: Any old towel or piece of sturdy rope will do the job.

Disc Toys

Consider frisbee, and you can probably immediately relate to having a lot of fun. This type of retrieving toy is fantastic for increasing energy expenditure, making them run, and getting those tiny hearts racing. This is a terrific way to get some much-needed cardio for all involved, as well as some one-on-one time together.

☐ The *ChuckIt Zipflight Flyer Dog Frisbee* is gentle on your companion's gums and teeth, similar to playing frisbee, and is perfect for long distance fetch.

☐ Outside of the curving top, the *Chuckit! Indoor Super Slider Dog Self Fetch Squeaker Toy* is virtually disc-shaped. This is a terrific, exciting toy for doggo, as it glides around the floor, causing them to chase and pounce on it. When they jump on it, it might squeal as well.

☐ *The ChuckIt Paraflight Flyer Dog Frisbee* is extremely light and can even float on water. It includes a nylon inner that is soft on doggo's teeth and gums, making it ideal for fetch.

☐ A DIY alternative: A simple frisbee still suffices for a lot of dog owners.

Treat Dispensing Toys

These toys involve some cognitive engagement from your dog, keeping them entertained while still feeding them. This is an excellent approach to guarantee that your pet has some mental stimulation while you are away; after all, aside from you, treats are what make their wee worlds go round.

- The *Treat Dispensing Bob-a-Lot Dog Toy* is a treat dispensing toy that entertains and feeds at the same time. It also works well in aiding to establish proper eating habits.

- The infamous *Kong Wobbler* is a very popular wobbly, spinning chew toy among dog owners, dispensing food and snacks that gets dispensed as soon as doggo's nose or paw pushes it which can keep them entertained for hours.

- A DIY alternative: You could use an empty 2 liter soda bottle and cut a few holes in it that would allow for the treats to pop out as doggo plays around with it.

Chew Toys

As previously said, some dogs enjoy noisy squeak toys while others avoid them in favor of a more soothing chew toy. Some dogs may become violent as a result of the squeaky sound and tear them apart, thus investing in a couple of them is a smart idea for those hounds who find them appealing.

- The *Hyper Pet Tennis Chewz Ring* is another favorite among dog owners because, in addition to being a chew toy, it also works well for fetch or tug.

- *Petstages Orka Dental Links* are three chewy interlinked rings that are an excellent long-lasting alternative to splintering sticks that may help divert destructive behavior.

- Because of its incredible resilience, the *Benebone Bacon Stick*, which is flavored with real bacon, is ideal for vigorous chewers. Its distinctive design requires some coordination to correctly sink the teeth in, making it excellent for mental stimulation.

- The *Mammoth Flossy Chews Color Rope Tug Toy* is a knotted piece of rope made of non-toxic Cotton-Poly yarn that is ideal for tug or retrieve.

- The *SPOT Colorful Rope Bungee Dog Toy* is yet another rope toy variation, and believe me, there is a wide range of rope toys available. Ones that are looped and knotted and are attached with balls, bottles, or plushies of various colors.

- A DIY alternative: A lovely old plushy, plaited rope, or the ever reliable tennis ball would all do the job.

In all honesty, there is no use in breaking your bank balance when acquiring your companion toys because these toys will almost always be damaged. There are many durable, low-cost options available, and your dog is unlikely to be aware of names, labels, or fancy packaging. Blessed with technology in our day and age, a lot of dog toys are robotic, working with apps, flickering lights and all, dispensers, balls you name it. These options tend to be a bit more on the pricier side however.

WHAT'S TOXIC?

Do you want to know something very profound?

Nobody regulates dog toys.

You read that correctly, there is barely any regulation. Don't despair; it's the same with pretty much anything we as humans use or consume in our daily lives. The only thing you can do about it is raise awareness of what is and is not acceptable. Read the fine print, which is frequently overlooked. It is well worth the effort and time to educate yourself about the "small print". Don't just blindly dive in and purchase the latest and greatest, and instead make educated decisions. You would not buy yourself a toxic object of any sort, why do that to doggo?

Yes, the general argument is that it does not seize life in a single day. There is some truth to that, but it is similar to a slow poison that gradually depletes the quality of life. That is why it is so crucial to understand what to look for;so let us now focus on the fine print.

Keep Your Eyes Peeled

The following substances are things that you should avoid, at best, be sure that it is minimal in your household when it comes to doggo.

- PVC, or polyvinyl chloride, is not dangerous to your dog in and of itself; what matters are the other substances that are added to it. As a result, unless you are an alchemist, it is best to avoid any toys that contain this substance.

- BPA, or bisphenol A, has caused a lot of controversy in the world of infant feeding bottles. As a result, don't be surprised if you see any infant feeding products labeled BPA-free, hence steer clear as much as possible.

- Phthalates is a type of additive found in many PVC products. This is extremely dangerous because it can damage the liver and kidneys.

- Melamine is not just something from a kitchen floor in the 60's, it is a substance that is still broadly used in various products today, aside from the health risks it poses. Some pet foods have even been recalled due to containing this substance. Thus, if you see the word melamine, it is best to decline.

- Lead is a problem that even we as humans must be extra cautious about in our diets and lives. This poison, which damages organs, the gastrointestinal tract, and the nervous system, leaves no room for compromise when it comes to health. Any indications of lead in any product should be avoided as much as possible.

- Bromine is another substance to be cautious of because it can cause digestive problems and difficulty urinating.

- Chromium is a type of insulin, but it can be extremely toxic and cause serious health problems such as cancer in humans. Consider the consequences for your dog.

- Oh, Arsenic, the focal point of so many murder mysteries. Should I even go on? Loss of consciousness, vomiting, and death would seal the deal on a ready supply of this toxin. A very big no-no.

- Formaldehyde is most commonly used as a preservative, particularly by taxidermists. This is a no-go zone due to the possibility of digestive and respiratory problems.

If you see any of this on a toy label, be cautious before reaching into your pockets and spending your hard-earned money. You do have options; you can make a habit of reading the fine print, or you can make your own toys. When you go the DIY route, at least you know what your doggo is eating, which eliminates the guessing game in terms of long-term consequences. Aside from this, you will be pleasantly surprised to see how many manufacturers out there share and are aware of the same concerns. Be sure to do your homework before you head on out and enjoy some "retail therapy" for the sake of doggo.

How much is too much when it comes to substances and toxins in pet toys?

Think twice before reaching for your wallet and if you see any of these things on a toy label. You have two choices: read the fine print to ensure you understand what you are purchasing, or make your own toys. You know exactly what your doggo is eating when you do it yourself, which eliminates the guessing game in terms of long-term consequences. Aside from that, you'll be surprised at how many manufacturers have the same concerns and are aware of them. As a result, there are healthier options available. Do your research before going out for some "retail therapy" for the sake of your doggo.

This is not a death threat, but rather something that should raise awareness. I repeat, use your own logic and discretion, because what works for one household may not work for another, because all of our needs, including doggos, differ. Toxins cannot be avoided in today's world unless you live in a self-contained bubble. The harsh reality is that consumerism has duped and compelled us into taking the easy and "time saving" route. But, in essence, what is the true cost of all of this? Is it really that simple? Sitting in a drive-thru line? Are these cool tricks and glowing sticks really making life easier?

At the end of the day, it's all about balance, not just in your own life, but also in your dog's. We all live once, and we are here to experience life in all its glory, including your doggo, so having some tech toys and some homemade ones would be fantastic. So, buy those glittery sparkly toys, make those hippy DIY ones. I encourage you to do so because, after all, variety is the spice of life, but awareness is key.

These are just the fundamentals of amusing your four-legged pal; let's continue for more training advice and inventive ways to keep your critter entertained.

CHAPTER 4:
TRAINING TIPS

MENTAL EXERCISE FOR DOGS

CHARLOTTE NELSON

Who says an old dog can't be taught new tricks? You can teach any dog, regardless of age, some basics.

There is no denying how much you love your Fido, but this love can become spread very thin if they lack obedience, which, as lady luck would have it, usually happens at the most inconvenient and unpredictable times. You can easily iron out these kinks by starting with simple obedience commands like sit, wait, and come when called.

This is beneficial not only because they will be better behaved or because you can show off your furry pal and all his tricks, but it also gives them more freedom to do things they enjoy. This could include accompanying you on additional visits to friends or simply running off the lead for a while, enjoying their freedom and independence. Aside from that, your doggo is a very evolutionary quirk who actually enjoys learning, especially with the obligatory little rewards which form part of the process.

Let's focus on some fundamental tips to keep in mind as you begin this "training rodeo" with your pal in order to dial down the volume on some of the overwhelm you may be feeling in terms of expectations.

TOP TRAINING TIPS

We all enjoy a good tip, and with the help of these, your magnificent mutt can perform some amazing tricks. The added bonus is that this is yet another opportunity for the two of you to strengthen your special bond.

Treats Are Tools

I suppose we have a better chance of selling ice to an Eskimo than finding a furry companion who refuses any kind of treat.

And, you guessed it, when it comes to training your mutt, treats are very effective tools that are ideal for encouraging good behavior or learning new ones. It goes without saying that this should not be your go-to method for getting your doggo to do what you want, so proceed with caution to avoid instilling the notion that there will be a treat around every corner for every action.

Patience Is a Virtue

Rome wasn't built in a day and neither is your Fido going to pick up on an onslaught of new tricks.

They do get tired, it is new to them, and your patience might falter at times. These or some of the facts, but if you can see that either your patience or their attention is adrift, take a break and proceed the following day. This will avoid the whole process from becoming a stressful endeavor for you and your mutt.

Consistency Is Key

As much as repetition is pivotal to you acquiring and instilling a new habit, it is no different when it comes to your pooch.

Maintain consistency in your training techniques by repeating the same exercise using the same technique to avoid confusion until the behavior or action is properly instilled in them. You should also incorporate training on a daily basis for it to be effective and begin producing proper results, so make it a part of your daily schedule and stick to it.

Ditch Distractions

Just like kids, teaching your pooch is not going to work if there are any distractions that might pull that little mind in a different direction.

Hide the toys and triggers to make it easier for that little peanut to focus. Keep in mind that their attention spans do have a time limit, so you should ideally keep these sessions sweet and short, about 10 to 15 minutes per day would suffice.

Keep It Simple

Your dog did not come with a "fully proficient in English" certification. Thus stick to simple words like sit, stay, no, and yes for instance.

With time you can elaborate and build onto these basics, but until they get to better understand the sounds, it's best to stick to the one worders.

Give It a Moment

Don't let your excitement run away with you if your furry friend doesn't immediately respond to a command.

Allow them a few minutes to process what they have just experienced. If, after five counts, you still get the "are you crazy human?" look, repeat the command and perhaps incorporate a hand gesture to help convey the message.

Gear Up

Make sure you have the necessary equipment on hand during your training sessions to help you run things more comfortably; after all, these things exist to make life easier for you and your doggo.

You don't have to go overboard and obtain all five star resources, a simple treat pouch and a comfy harness are two basic tools that can make life easier for the both of you.

Get Help

At times, your canine may require more training than your knowledge can provide, and enlisting professional assistance is unquestionably a good idea, allowing both you and your doggo to learn.

You will gain a lot of new information, training tips and tricks, and some very useful advice to help you continue your training journey well into the future.

Proof the Skill

You should not expect your snoot to behave and replicate any newfound skill outside of the environment in which they were first taught.

As a result, it is critical to gradually expose them to different environments and train them to execute that behavior. You have to proof the skill, expose the dynamic in different situations.

Be Aware

During training, keep an eye out for any signs of stress or anxiety. This is critical because if it is overlooked, all of your efforts will be futile, and your doggo will begin to exhibit signs of aggression and difficulty learning.

As a result, if you notice signs of distress, such as a tucked tail, cowering away from you, or pinned-back ears, take a break and play a game to avoid amplifying the stress, anxiety, and overwhelm.

Don't Bribe

Now, I mentioned that treats are the currency of the trade, but there is a fine line between treats being a reward and treats becoming a bribe. Stay away from the latter.

Your snoot should be kept guessing as to whether or not they will receive a treat; it should not be a given every time. Keep them guessing by gradually reducing the frequency with which you distribute the rewards.

A significant achievement would be when they can perform a variety of tricks one after the other without requiring that treat as reinforcement. However, you must always give a treat at some point; never completely abstain from awarding treats.

Time Those Treats

This will require you to practice your treat timing. You must be consistent with your rewarding system.

If they perform a trick, do not make them sit and wait for the treat; instead, give it to them as soon as possible, along with praise. Maintain consistency in this timing so that they can form an association with the trick as a positive behavior.

End Well

Since they have fought so hard to win your favor, you must always conclude each session with a spectacular finale for your dear companion.

Play with them, pet them, or provide a special treat to reinforce the idea that training is joyful and exciting for them.

What Works

Dogs, like their human counterparts, are all unique, and what might work great for one woofer might not stick well with another at all.

Maybe your doggo would rather be caressed than rewarded with a goodie after each performance. Know what makes their hearts beat and how they respond in order to know what to give as rewards and reinforcements, as well as where you should make some adjustments throughout training.

These are just a few pointers to get the show started for the two of you. As with any exercise, begin slowly and gradually increase your progress. Remember that training is more than just teaching new skills; it also keeps your beloved Fido happy.

Unlike us complicated humans with so many desires, all your snoot needs checked off their little list is spending some time with you, a couple of treats, and some new tricks to feel a sense of independence.

CHAPTER 5:
POSITIVE REINFORCEMENT, NOT PUNISHMENT

MENTAL EXERCISE FOR DOGS

CHARLOTTE NELSON

L ooking into a furry person's eyes reveals an abundance of warmth and love that leaves much for humans to aspire to.

With a soul like that, it is essential to comprehend the method of instruction you are utilizing in order to preserve the happiness in those young pupils' eyes. And the good news is that the practice of positive reinforcement exists.

Reinforcement occurs when you increase or encourage a specific type of behavior. Punishment, on the other hand, indicates that you are reducing or discouraging a particular type of behavior. However, we will not limit ourselves to this simple explanation; instead, we will delve deeper into the science of animal learning.

So, to begin, let's define operant conditioning in order to better understand how those gears respond to impulses from the world around them.

OPERANT CONDITIONING

Your doorbell rings again, and old foo-foo joins in with a bark, assaulting your poor ears. Now, why does your doggo always react in this manner?

It is due to a phenomenon known as classical conditioning, or associative learning, in which there is a trigger and an association is formed with it. In this case, doggo has associated the ringing doorbell with humans arriving, hence the excitement. This is a more involuntary type of learning that occurs, based solely on the association of circumstances that happen on a regular basis by chance.

Operant conditioning, in contrast, is when you start spending time and training your mongrel and behavior is connected to a consequence. Therefore, if you give your fido a treat, the gears in his little mind will link the behavior as positive, and if you take away his toy, the association will be negative. These two distinct activities either promote or discourage certain behaviors, or they raise or lower their frequency. Keep in mind that it's only addition and subtraction; do not consider it in terms of good and bad.

THE FOUR QUADRANTS

Operant conditioning can be divided into four quadrants, each of which has specific effects on your doggo's behavior.

First Quadrant: Positive Reinforcement

This is simply the old reward system in action. Because the word positive is associated with adding something in this quadrant, you would like to reinforce or encourage a certain behavior, which will lead to an increase in that specific behavior.

You give your mutt a treat if you say "paw" and they give you that furry claw. The end result? They will repeat this as reinforcement because of the reward encouraging this specific behavior.

Second Quadrant: Positive Punishment

Now you have to hold it together because we have the word positive, which means you are adding something again.

However, there is a negative word here as well, punishment, and this refers to adding something negative, something your canine will dislike, such as a spank, to prevent the specific behavior from being repeated for instance.

Third Quadrant: Negative Reinforcement

Negative implies taking something away, so something will be taken away in this case to promote a specific behavior.

You're probably attempting to interpret this one. If you start yanking on the leash to stop your doggo from misbehaving while out for a walk, as soon as you let up because they calmed down you are letting go of the negative, and your companion has most likely learned to listen and will most likely comply the next time. Hence, you are creating something negative and will remove it if they comply to reinforce a specific behavior.

Fourth Quadrant: Negative Punishment

Yes, as you suspected, you are taking something away to deter a particular behavior. As you would if a youngster misbehaved and you took away their toy.

Doggo would learn that you do not support their behavior if you ignore them when they are biting your hand, depriving them of the attention they crave and decreasing the likelihood that they will repeat it for instance.

And which of these four quadrants do you think ranks highest in terms of educating your fluffy fur ball?

POSITIVE REINFORCEMENT

Positive reinforcement is where your attention should be directed. This is not to say that the other methods aren't effective; however, most dog trainers focus on positive reinforcement while interspersing it with negative punishment.

In my opinion, these are simply more humane, because incorporating any negative connotations into training can deter your doggo from the actual training process, or worse, create some animosity towards you and erode your bond.

It is all about the positive things with positive reinforcement, and the beauty of this is that it encourages doggo to become an active participant in the entire process. This approach also works wonders in removing the fear of doing something wrong, making them more willing to try new things. By focusing on the positive, they will have a stronger awareness of what to do rather than what not to do, resulting in a significantly more successful behavioral outcome.

This approach will also keep their interest piqued, as they will be constantly on the lookout for new treats, providing them with more cognitive stimulation. The best part is that your bond will grow stronger because you will be associated with treats!

CHAPTER 6:
TRAINING MISTAKES

MENTAL EXERCISE FOR DOGS

CHARLOTTE NELSON

Nobody is perfect, especially when it comes to trying something new for the first time. And let's be honest, dog training is not always a walk in the park. This should not deter you from venturing out and taking on new challenges, because a little bit of advice can go a long way.

There are as many pitfalls that many owners fall into when it comes to training their canine companion as there are tricks and advice out there, which can cause quite a bit of frustration on both ends of the leash.

We'll look at some of the red flags you should be aware of in order to avoid some of the significant negative consequences they could have on doggo and your training efforts.

WHAT TO AVOID

Here are some actions you should sidestep when rehearsing with your woofer:

Futile Repetition

You can not draw blood from a stone. Stop and reassess if you notice your companion is not responding to a specific training method.

Of course, these cues you are instilling will not take hold overnight, so any new introductions should be given some time to take effect. The amount of time varies depending on the difficulty of the trick and your dog's personality, but you can expect it to take anywhere from four to seven weeks to become fully established.

At the end of the day, you are the best judge of your canine companion and can tell if there is any progress. If nothing happens after a certain amount of time, you must change your approach and try different methods.

Not Practicing Outside of Training

You already understand the importance of consistency and the importance of incorporating training into your daily routine; however, incorporating it outside of sessions will help further instill the behavior.

This will also help in gradually introducing them to the required action in a variety of settings. You could simply say "paw" while sitting and relaxing, for example to incorporate it into your normal routine.

Cue Nagging

Nagging is a problem, and in the dog world nagging occurs when you repeat cues. "Come, come, come" is a well-known phrase. And have you noticed that when you do this, doggo does not always respond as you would like?

What to do?

You are only supposed to give a cue once, and if your fido does not respond after giving them a few minutes, you should try to get their attention through a hand movement instead of repeating the same word over and over again. The only thing this repetition does is teaching doggo that an immediate response is not required when the que is heard.

The aim of the game is to teach your mutt to respond to a single cue.

Not Focusing

Do not be surprised, because many people mistake training for a good social catch-up with friends or a good time for scrolling on their smartphones.

Training your companion necessitates a considerable dedication and your undivided attention. As a result, you should give that period your complete focus, put the phone down, or plan another social activity. The best course of action is to stay focused on the task at hand in order to see the desired results because your buddy is as sharp as a sword and will immediately pick up on this energy.

A Trick at a Time

This is not a human school where a variety of disciplines may be taught in a single day; even humans struggle with this concept at the best of times.

Avoid teaching more than one trick at a time; this will not only take them a protracted time to learn, but will also cause a lot of confusion and frustration.

Pick it and stick to it— one trick at a time.

Begin with simple tricks and work your way up to more advanced ones, and remember that patience is a virtue.

Training Moods

If you or your doggo are feeling jittery or under the weather, postpone the training session until everyone has healed and returned to their normal selves.

Downtime could be spent bonding in various other ways.

Don't Chase

When your sploot with the snoot runs off in a specific direction, do not pursue them in order to retrieve them. Please excuse the pun, but you are not the retriever.

Stay calm and call them back by name, whistle, or whatever recall command you use as long as they are still in sight. If you don't stick to your guns in this case, they'll think it's a big old chase game, and recovering from this incorrectly perceived amount of fun will be challenging.

One Doggo, One Trainer

If you are training your pet, it should be completely reserved for you. Others stepping in and taking over will confuse your mut and lengthen the learning period.

It's great to get some advice now and then, but this is a line that must not be crossed. If your dog has a professional trainer, find out what methods you can use at home to reinforce their teachings without causing confusion.

Refrain From Using the Name

Using your heart beat at your feet's name when reprimanding them is an absolute no-no.

This is harmful because it creates a negative connotation and much confusion; a simple two-letter word, "no," would suffice. When positive reinforcement is needed, use that well-known name.

Cue Poisoning

Avoid using cues you use for something your four-legged pal doesn't like, especially in the early stages of training.

Perhaps doggo dislikes having his ivories brushed, so when you use the cue "sit" they may make the assumption that it's "ivory time" and hesitation sets in.

These are just a few of the things to keep an eye out for. We touched on some points in the previous chapter, but here's a quick recap to refresh your memory:

- Too long training sessions

- Untimely delivery of treats

- Being inconsistent with cues, training, or treats

- Harsh discipline

Another critical aspect is recognizing when your sploot is tired; let's take a look at some tell-tale signs of this.

IT'S TIME TO END

When one is concentrating or having fun, time appears to be non-existent. As a result, it's easy to overlook when the star of your show has had enough and could use some T.L.C. and shut-eye.

Keep an eye out for the following signs to see if your snooty sploot needs to take a break from serious leveling up:

Unable to Hold Positions

Basically, when the pitter-patter of feet and body wobbles begin, their body has had enough for the day.

This indicates a drop in energy levels, and when this occurs, you can forget about any outstanding performances. Weight shifting, difficulty holding positions, and difficulty keeping their feet stationary are all signs that it's time to take a break.

Grumbles

If there is some grumbling or sneering rearing its ugly head, it cannot be stated more emphatically that it is time to stop.

This is your mutt's way of telling you that they're tired and starting to get frustrated.

Turning Down Treats

Oh no! That did not just happen! Treats don't seem to possess the same power they use to?

You need no neon lights now to let you know that it's time to relax. This could be because doggo is full and has had enough treats, or because doggo is literally short-circuiting, in which their coordination begins to deteriorate and they lack deliberate movements.

Efforts to Retreat

When those eyes are wandering around with a mission, they are in actual fact looking for an escape route, a way to exit the "party".

This is yet another indication that they are tired and should leave the training environment. Be on the lookout for other calming signals, such as a flick of their tongue, or they may simply walk away, leaving you to wonder what you did wrong if you weren't aware.

Because you are the most familiar with your pooch, you will be able to tell when they are tired or have lost interest. When this occurs, you could take a short break and resume training by undertaking a new exercise, or you could completely discontinue training for the day and finish with a good round of playtime.

Let's talk about socializing with children and how your companion can be trained to be as gentle and caring with kids as they are with you.

CHAPTER 7:
PLAYING WITH KIDS

For folks that already have the pitter-patter of little human feet who want to adopt a doggo, or for folks who already have the pitter-patter of paws who want to become parents, and even for folks that prefer only the pitter-patter of paws, childproofing is necessary.

Even though they are still human, which might seem debatable at times, children appear to be very different from adults when it comes to dogs. They are louder, obviously smaller, unpredictable, and can be aggressive at times; they smell different too. As a result, your dog may be startled to encounter a "foreign" being as such for the first time.

As important as house training your wonderful mutt is, so is childproofing them. This is why basic training is so important, because you will never be able to childproof your pet if they have not yet learned basic control commands such as "sit" or "down".

CHILDPROOFING DOGGO

It is a warm emotion evoking thought to think of all the love in one room with kids and dogs in the mix, and they do make a great combo at times, but only if doggo knows how to behave and interact around them.

Now, there are two types of dogs: those who love children and those who do not. Regardless of which category your mutty pal falls into, they still require proper training and socialization to understand the boundaries in order to ensure safe interaction. The same rings true for children as well; however, we are delving into doggo territory with this book.

Some dogs are truly afraid of children and should be trained to understand their boundaries in order to keep any interaction at a distance, because one never knows if they might get startled, making the unsurety of the situation too risky.

If you do not have children, you must always ensure that children who visit are safe around your dog and vice versa, while keeping your eyes on all the prizes.

Obedience Program

When it comes to childproofing your dog, one of the first steps you should take is to teach them basic commands.

Another option is to enroll in dog training classes, which would be a great way to further reinforce socialization by exposing your dog to other dogs.

No Jumping

Jumping may be a way for you and your doggo to interact, but it can be dangerous for children, who can easily be knocked over and injured to varying degrees.

However, it is best to curb that enthusiasm and not encourage jumping at all, instead command them to sit or discourage the behavior through proper training methods.

Socialize

Exposing your pet to social situations is important from the outset. Although it is simpler to do and for them to adjust when they are younger, senior dogs may still be socially integrated; it will simply take a little longer to establish some form of equilibrium.

A warm, cuddly puppy brings true joy, so having people fawn over them and absorbing all the attention makes it much simpler to adjust to socializing. With an older companion you would have to proceed a lot slower, and be sure to lather on the praise along with plenty of treats.

Just be sure, whether young or old, to immediately remove them from a given social situation at any first indications of distress.

Be a Kid

Kids run, they jump, they're loud and lively, and they're nothing like adults. As a result, it is recommended that you occasionally let your hair down and do the same.

Yes, you read that correctly: you should run around the yard, jump around, and make a lot of noise while cueing doggo to stay seated. This will most certainly put a big smile on your dial. Another option is to take your four-legged friend to a playground to interact with children up close and personal.

Don't just pitch up and put your fido in the spotlight; start from a distance and work your way closer each day to avoid them becoming overwhelmed.

Handling Exercises

All that furry cuteness is inarguably irresistible, thus you can not blame anyone for wanting to tickle, cuddle, and tug at that companion of yours.

Start by incorporating similar handling such as tugging at the tail or ears, hugging and picking up the paws, all of course gently. Praise and rewards are standard as usual when introducing anything new, but if you notice any signs of distress or anxiety, it is best to keep kids at bay.

Hello Kids Toys

All that furry cuteness is undeniably irresistible, so no one can blame them for wanting to tickle, cuddle, and tug at your companion.

Begin by gently incorporating similar handling such as tugging at the tail or ears, hugging, and picking up the paws, very gently of course. When introducing anything new, praise and rewards are standard, but if you notice any signs of distress or anxiety, it is best to keep children at bay for future reference.

As a result, introducing them to children's toys allows you to reinforce commands such as "leave", as well as train them to redirect their attention back to their own stash of toys.

Don't Force It

Never, ever hold your dog so that a child can pet him or her as a method of introduction. Dogs should always approach children on their own terms and at their own pace, without forcing the situation.

This appears to be a forced introduction for your companion, which could be a frightening experience for them. Biting, growling, or snapping may result as an attempt to avoid the perceived threat.

Crate Training

Crate training is a great way to establish a safe place for your woofer. When they become overstimulated and have had enough, they know they have a safe space which they can retreat to and take some time out.

Just make sure to inform your little human visitors that doggo's crate should not be tampered with or played with, and that it is completely off limits.

Positive Reinforcement

Be sure to keep that positive reinforcement pouring in when it comes to your mutt being in the presence of children.

Reward good behavior with, yet again, treats and keep those compliments rolling in, this will help them establish a connection that good things happen when children are around.

Talk to the Kids

Every home has its rules and ought to be respected by all that cross the threshold. Therefore, it's crucial to establish boundaries early on when it comes to doggo in order to prevent any ambiguity and unwelcome situations.

- Do not approach the dog when he is eating or chewing anything.
- Do not disturb the dog when he is sleeping or resting.
- Do not force attention or any interaction with the dog.
- When you speak to, or pet the dog, use caution and be gentle.
- The dog's crate is off limits, that is their special place.
- Children should never ever be left alone with a dog, an adult should always be present.
- Teach the children some basic commands such as "sit".

PREPARING DOGGO FOR A VISIT WITH KIDS

Remember that varying ages of humans appear to dogs as separate species. With this in mind, it is critical to check in with your trusted pal and act as their facilitator; after all, you are also a parent, and the welfare and responsibility of your overly hairy child falls squarely on your shoulders.

If your companion becomes overly excited when guests arrive, keep him isolated in his crate or a room until the nerves, excitement, and guests have settled down. Introduce your children to your four-legged companion by giving them treats to offer doggo; this is an excellent way to establish a positive association right away. Speaking of positive associations, don't forget to adore your snoot as much as you adore the children in order to avoid any feelings or associations of being excluded or ignored.

The interaction between youngsters and your beloved pet should always be supervised by an adult because both species can be unexpected. Keep your dog's leash on even better so that you can swiftly regain control in an emergency.

Always be on the lookout for signs from your furry friend that can suggest they need to relax or that they are feeling agitated.

You don't have to be like "octo-mom" to ensure that everything is fine between doggo and kids; all that is required is proper training, precautions, and supervision. Check these boxes and you and your mut will be good to go when it comes to hitting the social scene.

Here's where it gets fun—games galore! I assure you that there are many more activities for your fantastical foo-foo to engage in than testing the mailman.

CHAPTER 8:
FUN AND GAMES

We investigated the advantages of keeping your dog mentally and physically fit so that you can get the most out of each other.

Even though playing and learning are enjoyable activities, not all games are created equal. So, before you rush in to have some fun, make sure you understand the impact the games you're playing have on your beloved snoot. Interestingly, some undesirable behaviors that dogs pick up on can be traced back to when they were puppies, implying that what you choose to play with them has a direct impact on their behavior. Yes, you should be aware of the game's objective to prevent encouraging undesirable behavior among your participants.

A very important point to emphasize is that your four-legged companion is like a sponge, and everything you do teaches them something that they pick up on.

So, how do you play, learn, and exercise?

Let us take a look.

GAMES TO PLAY

The goal of training your pooch is for them to be able to exercise self-control, so playing structured games should be your primary focus.

To get the most out of playtime, you must engage in the appropriate games and exercises that will get those little gears turning and churning in your companion's head, improving their obedience and listening skills.

Search is a fantastic example of this type of game. Doggo gets to look for toys and treats, which requires them to use their senses, pay attention, and think a lot. Another excellent choice is the ever-popular fetch game, which reinforces cues, obedience, and sharpens canine retrieval skills.

Here are a few more examples of sure-fire games to get that little heart and mind racing:

- Training and tricks to improve their behavior and sense of independence.

- Walks to explore and have different stimulation through experiencing new things.

- Puzzle toys, but make sure to have more than one that you rotate out on a regular basis to keep things interesting.

- When it comes to having a happy heart and a happy mind, quality time in any relationship reigns supreme.

- Socialization is as important for your dog as it is for you, so make time to meet and greet new animals, places, and people.

GAMES TO PROCEED WITH CAUTION

The amount of playing, jumping, and running can differ from breed to breed, however when it comes to these four-legged mutts, this is all pretty standard.

The most important thing to remember during any playing, exercising, or teaching is to maintain control at all times, and it is sometimes best to avoid some games that will cause your pooch to become overly excited and carried away, because this can more often than not encourage aggressive behavior.

Avoid any games that require you to use parts of your body, such as your hands or your clothing. Tug of war is another game that should be avoided; in fact, anything that causes growling and biting should be avoided because it may positively reinforce these types of undesirable negative behaviors.

When they start getting out of hand, the best thing you can do is stop the game, cue it with a "no", and walk away to teach them that they went too far and that the behavior is unacceptable.

KEEP THIS IN MIND

Dogs differ in the same way that humans do; you may enjoy a game of tennis while your human companion may feel as if they are on a battlefield.

Let's put this into "dog world" terms. You might have a dog who gets overly excited or overwhelmed and enjoys barking and lunging. As a result, your dog is not an off-leash play candidate in parks, and to keep your critter entertained, some free running and a round of flirt pole play in the backyard, for example, would be ideal.

Maybe you have a more reserved hound who is very possessive of their toys and any attempt to initiate play is met with a growl. The better option would be to engage in some nose work in which doggo must seek out treats or objects with various scents. As a result, that little personality comes into play when selecting games to ensure you are triggering the right mental processes.

Here are a few pointers to remember:

You Are Not the Toy

Avoid making yourself the target of any game because this will encourage undesirable behavior such as biting and growling at people.

Use Your Posture

Having said that, your posture speaks volumes to doggo. When things start to get wild and exciting, make sure you're taller than your companion by standing up and cuing them to be still. Stay calm and use your cues if they act like a little thief and try to steal something from you, such as toys or food. Also be sure to watch your tone, when playing, your voice should be up-beat and encouraging.

Never become hysterical, and never take a submissive stance such as pulling away or raising objects above your head; doing so will only encourage jumping and chasing. Maintain your position, remain calm, keep toys below the waist, and redirect the behavior.

Know Your Toys

Yes, variety is the spice of life, which is why we appreciate a wide range of toys. When it comes to toys, knowing what to use and when to use it is critical when playing with doggo.

Ladies and gentlemen, you have pacifier toys which are used to ward them off your furniture and shoes, which refers to chew toys. Your other category would be interactive toys that are used for games in general, such as the squeaky ones or moving ones, like balls for instance.

Playing Is Learning

Remember that they are sponges, so whatever game you are playing, including your reactions throughout the entire play session, is information you are feeding that canine mind, so even if it is playtime, keep your cool, be wary, and make sure you establish that you are in control. Keep it fun, but don't break the speed limit with regards to excitement to the point where there is no impulse control.

Keep It Novel

You need to be in control of which toys are played with and when, so avoid leaving all toys lying around where doggo can get to them whenever he wants. Pack away the interactive toys until needed; you get to decide what is played and when it ends, you are the alpha.

Spay for Play

You should definitely think about neutering or spaying your furry friend. This simple procedure will assist your dog in better regulating those domineering impulses, making play much more enjoyable for all parties involved.

Play Often

Try to fit in as much play time as possible, and make sure to do so in a variety of settings, such as at home, the park, or the backyard.

It's also natural for doggo to initiate play. Proceed with caution, however, because you don't want your companion to believe he is the alpha. To avoid this scenario, when your pup approaches you to play a game, respond with a control cue first, such as "down" or "sit", then toss the toy after doggo is compliant. This act will be rewarding in and of itself for doggo.

Here are some suggestions for making exercise, training, and playing more enjoyable. It could be a little difficult at first, but once these treaties are made, playtime will go without a hitch as boundaries are established.

Let's jump right in and explore the various games you may play both indoors and outdoors to keep that mind and hairy body in shape. Not just for doggo but for you too, after all, according to conventional wisdom, if you are overweight, it is likely that your doggo isn't getting enough playtime.

CHAPTER 9:
FOOD GAMES

MENTAL EXERCISE FOR DOGS

CHARLOTTE NELSON

Most games feature treats, but in this one, they'll take center stage. Now, if you want to witness tenacity and resilience in action, food games are most definitely going to do it. The large "can do" egos that are in play are amusing, but the real charm is in how it boosts their confidence, which may also be calming for others. When you have more than one pooch gracing you with their presence at home, it is highly recommended that you separate these toys in order to avoid fights and allow them to truly hone in and focus on the game, rather than feeling protective and hasty over it.

According to one study, food enrichment toys, which perform the same function as food games, increase activity, decrease barking frequency, and stimulate appetite (Schipper et al. 2008). Aside from that, food games can serve as excellent safety cues as well.

Let's look into some creative ways you can get the ball rolling.

GAMES

Dog Lollies

Let's start simple; I'm sure your folks used to make you something similar, ice lollies. This literal taste explosion is an easy, cost effective DIY option for working your snoots' mental abilities while cooling their bodies down and providing nourishment, especially great for summer days.

How To:

Location- this game may be conducted both indoors and outdoors.

1. *Combine your dog's favorite treats or food with broth. Water will suffice.*

2. *Chicken broth appears to be popular, and using broth adds extra nutrients.*

3. *Pour the mixture into a container or ice tray, depending on the size of your fur ball, and place it in the freezer.*

4. *Allow your companion to enjoy the process of the flavorful ice melting and slipping around by giving them one piece at a time.*

The Apple Puzzle

An apple a day keeps doggo at play and this novel method is a great alternative to the ever-popular kong toy, so it's worth a shot.

How To:

Location- this game may be conducted both indoors and outdoors.

1. *You will most certainly need an apple for this.*

2. *Remove the core of the apple in order to create a hollow center.*

3. *Stuff it with some flavorful treats.*

4. *Voila, let doggo enjoy rolling, chewing, and eating away.*

Sniffle Mat

Aside from keeping that mind active, this is a great soothing game, especially for fussy eaters, and the added bonus is that you can easily make one yourself.

How To:

Location- this game may be conducted both indoors and outdoors.

1. *You will need a meshed rubber mat, and a fleece blanket.*

2. *Cut the fleece blanket into strips that are about 35 cm long and 5cm wide.*

3. *Thread each piece into the mesh mat separately and knot it so that the loose ends face upward, creating a fluffy textured carpet.*

4. *You can make this as dense as you prefer.*

5. *Place the treats in between the fluff and let doggo enjoy it.*

Kibble Count

This is a lovely guessing game, and you would find it rather fascinating if doggo starts catching on and understanding what the game is all about because this is a great cue training game.

How To:

Location- this game may be conducted both indoors and outdoors.

1. *You'll need some kibbles or other treats to get your dog excited and interested.*
2. *Hold 4 pieces of treats in one hand and 2 in the other.*
3. *Tell your furry friend to sit.*
4. *Keep your hands closed and arm's length away from the doggo.*
5. *Say "small" as you open your hands to reveal the treats, then close them again.*
6. *Wait for your companion to respond and pick a hand.*
7. *If the correct hand is picked, the treats are the prize.*
8. *Doggo will eventually get the hang of it with practice and patience.*
9. *Alternate between hands and cues such as "left" and "right" for instance.*

Obstacle Course

Remember when you were a kid and you used to make mazes and indoor tents out of blankets and chairs? This is very similar, right down to the levels of excitement you're used to when playing this game.

How To:

Location- this game may be conducted both indoors and outdoors.

1. *You'll need boxes, crates, or anything else that can be used to make a makeshift obstacle course.*

2. *To shake things up, add a kid's pool or something similar with sand or water.*

3. *Pack and arrange all of your items to create an obstacle course for your companion to explore and enjoy.*

4. *Use a treat to guide them through the course to familiarize them with it and demonstrate how it works.*

5. *Then scatter more treats throughout the course and let doggo explore.*

Shell Game

You'll notice that many of these games are very similar to ones we humans enjoyed at some point in our lives, and possibly still do. You will be the magician here, and entertain that snoot of yours as follows:

How To:

Location-this game may be conducted both indoors and outdoors.

1. *You'll need some plastic cups as well as some treats.*

2. *Begin by using only one cup and placing it face down on the ground with a treat inside.*

3. *Start off by cueing doggo to sit.*

4. *Then cue doggo to take it.*

5. *Doggo will try to get to the treat by knocking over the cup.*

6. *Then add another cup, but make sure doggo can see every time you hide a treat.*

7. *Do not move the cups until your companion understands the game.*

8. *If you notice that the fur ball understands how things work, you can increase the difficulty and begin shifting the cups around.*

The Burrito

Yet another great option to get your snoot sniffling and figuring things out. The towel burrito is a simple and inexpensive way to teach your dog new tricks like wiping his paws or cueing him to unroll the towel.

How To:

Location- this game may be conducted both indoors and outdoors.

1. *You will need a towel and yet again some treats.*

2. *Scatter some treats on an open towel.*

3. *Roll the towel up like a burrito, or any other shape that is preferable.*

4. *And give the surprise package to doggo to figure out how to unroll it and reach those treats.*

These are just a few examples that won't cost you a fortune, are simple to make, and have enormous positive effects on your dog's mental and physical health.

If you want to supplement the contents of the toy chest, there are numerous food toys available for dogs, including the Kong, Buster Cube, Atomic Treat Ball, and various other additional choices like food puzzles for instance. Try substituting various goodies, like bits of liver, if there is no sign of interest. Just make sure that all toys, whether they are made at home or bought from a store, are secure and won't choke your creature. Thus it's best to always have your canine enjoy these games supervised.

You must take immediate possession of the game or toy and, in the best case scenario, get in touch with a professional behaviorist if your dog exhibits any aggressive behavior against you or other people when given food games or toys.

CHAPTER 10:
HUNTING GAMES

Your dog's gene pool can be traced back to an apex hunting predator, the wolf. Many of these furry four-legged creatures have been bred and developed over time for other purposes, such as companionship. However, there will always be a wolf hiding deep within that little heart.

For some breeds, such as those with hunting instincts, this little wolf in the heart is much larger because it is fueled by extra endurance and stamina.

If you own a hunting dog, such as a hound or spaniel, you must accept one fact: hunting dogs hunt instinctively, and there is no way to change this fact. Thus, participating in hunting games is a great way to stimulate these deep-seated instincts and keep them mentally satiated. This is supported by research in which scientists threw a ball at some wolf puppies and were astounded by what happened: the wolf pups not only chased the ball, but also excitedly returned it to a person. The researchers went on to say that these types of behaviors could have aided in early dog domestication (Hansen Wheat & Temrin. 2020).

You will undoubtedly come up short in this situation if we had to compare your scenting skills to those of your fluffer, there is no disputing that. As a result, it is crucial to keep the mind and that sensitive sense active because it is fantastic physical activity and does wonders to reduce separation anxiety.

But any old dog can play hunting games, regardless of breed, so let's have a look at some alternatives.

GAMES

Dinner Time Hunt

By deviating from the usual dinner time ritual, you can keep that person's mind engaged. Depending on what suits you best, you can play this game with a homemade toy or one that you purchase. Even better, change up the toys to keep things exciting.

How To:

Location- this game may be conducted both indoors and outdoors.

1. *You'll need a favorite food toy, like a food puzzle, or you can just arrange the snacks in nice little piles.*

2. *Make sure it is a little portion because you do not want your doggo to become overly satisfied with treats.*

3. *Set these up all over the house.*

4. *When you are ready, just before meal time, hide doggo's meal as well.*

5. *There is no doubt that your pet will find this to be the most thrilling mealtime experience.*

Hide and Seek

With this one, you will be the "prey" therefore I can assure you that you will enjoy it just as much as your doggo.

How To:

Location- this game may be conducted both indoors and outdoors.

1. *You could ask a partner or friend to keep your snoot in check while you find a hiding spot. As an alternative, you may cue doggo to sit until you've hidden.*

2. *Be sure to have some treats on you to be sure your companion gets a reward for finding you.*

3. *As they say, the rest is history. Either you or your companion can cue doggo to find you.*

4. *Until your dog becomes used to the game, just remain hidden in the same location. Then, you can increase the difficulty by hiding in different spots.*

Fetch

Classic games are always a winner, thus they have stood the test of time, and fetch is most definitely top of the list for most fur balls. Burning some serious calories and keeping that mind focused, you will not only provide doggo with a healthy body and mind, but a happy heart too. It is preferable to play fetch outside because there is ample running space; however, a lighter version of fetch could be enjoyed indoors as well with a smaller ball and less power in the throw.

How To:

Location- this game may be conducted both indoors and outdoors.

1. *You'll need a ball, frisbee, or any other tossable favorite toy.*

2. *Toss the toy as far as you can.*

3. *But here's the catch: while doggo runs off to fetch it, you might as well do some sit ups or lunges. How's that for making the most of your time?*

4. *Always remember to greet doggo with a cue like "sit" or "give" upon return.*

5. *You can add a twist by playing scented fetch. Simply rub your doggo's toy with his favorite treats or food to give off a scent and toss it without doggo seeing where it lands, then cue "fetch".*

6. *Another option is to roll the ball or object rather than throw it; this is a simple way to alternate things.*

Word Hunt

This is a game that will require some patience and time to learn, but it is probably one of the best ones you can incorporate to expand your fur ball's vocabulary.

How To:

Location- this game may be conducted both indoors and outdoors.

1. *You would not need anything aside from the existing toy collection your mutt already reigns over.*

2. *Take one toy and repeat it's name to doggo, such as "kitty" for instance.*

3. *Then place the toy somewhere in the room and cue doggo to fetch "kitty".*

4. *Continue doing this until it becomes a habit.*

5. *Remove the toy from the room and repeat the whole exercise with a different toy.*

6. *If doggo understands the names of two toys, play the game with both by placing them somewhere in the room and asking him to fetch either one.*

7. *As previously stated, patience is required.*

Again, there are plenty of toys on the market that you can buy to use during any of these games. Not only that, but games like the shell game can help to stimulate those hunting instincts.

When playing these games, make sure to avoid encouraging any undesirable behaviors such as jumping and biting, as hunting games have a tendency to get some doggos overly excited. Always keep an eye on your dog's body language and behavior, especially for growling and aggressive barking in order to not instill these behaviors to form as part of their personalities.

CHAPTER 11:
SCENT GAMES

Getting your dog's nose to work every day with a little nosework, such as scent games, is extremely important.

Of course, you're thinking, because he smells with it. True, but once you understand how much this snout affects his daily life, you'll realize how important it is to improve this aspect. When it comes to smell, your four-footer is in a completely different realm than you are used to. This sense of theirs, in fact, is so strong that it would put any fragrance tester to shame.

When it comes to smell, your dog is in a completely different realm than you are used to. Surprisingly, one distinction exists, and that is in how they breathe. In contrast to humans, who inhale and exhale through both nostrils, your dog uses one for breathing and the other to send smells directly to their olfactory sensing region, which contains millions of receptors (Jenkins et al. 2018).

Aside from bolstering your dog's confidence, putting this sense to work, detecting scent and tracking down the source, stimulates the natural hunting instinct that dwells within every four-footed fur ball.

Let's roll along and look into some scent games that will contribute to cultivating your companion's talent.

GAMES

The Muffin Tin

This is a popular game that is excellent for teaching slow feeding.

How To:

Location- this game may be conducted both indoors and outdoors.

1. *Gather a muffin tin and some tennis balls.*

2. *Place the treats in the muffin tin molds. You can fill all of the molds with treats or just a few.*

3. *Tennis balls should be used to cover the molds.*

4. *Let doggo uncover the hidden treats through removing the tennis balls.*

5. *It might get rough, so you might have to hold the tin down at times.*

Box Search

Similar to the shell game, this is a simple scent game to get your doggo started, and you can progress to more advanced options from here.

How To:

Location- this game may be conducted both indoors and outdoors.

1. *You will require some empty boxes. Consider the size of your dog in relation to the box you will be using.*

2. *Arrange the boxes on the floor and pop a treat into some.*

3. *You can arrange these boxes in whichever way you like.*

4. *Allow doggo to dig in and enjoy selecting the appropriate box containing the beloved treats.*

5. *Remember to reward your dog when the treat treasure is discovered.*

6. *It is preferable to begin without closing or covering the boxes; as doggo becomes more familiar with the game, you can begin to incorporate this aspect.*

7. *Instead of leaving doggo to continue searching, lure him away from the game with another treat so he can tell when the game is over.*

Scent Hunt

Want to play a game that will teach your four-footer to become an expert tracker? Then scent hunt should be top on the list for you, as it is one of the methods that a lot of dog trainers use to train sniffer dogs as a matter of fact. It could be a bit tricky initially, thus patience would most definitely be required here. It is further recommended to start with a scent trail game before jumping into this option.

How To:

Location- this game may be conducted both indoors and outdoors.

1. *A scented toy will be required. This could be accomplished by rubbing a favorite treat scent onto one of doggo's toys.*

2. *Put the toy in a box, any box will do, a shoe box would be perfect.*

3. *Cue your pet to go find the toy.*

4. *If doggo finds the toy, the usual praise routine must be followed in order to establish the behavior.*

5. *As doggo gains a better understanding of the game, you can use more boxes to raise the stakes.*

6. *To avoid the other boxes becoming scented, keep the toy in the same box you initially placed it in.*

7. *When your clever mutt has mastered stage two, you can remove the scented toy and replace it with a strip of similar scented paper that you place in the same box that the toy was in.*

8. *Stage three would entail hiding the original toy in its box somewhere completely different, possibly even outside.*

9. *Wash your hands thoroughly and grab a new toy to keep on you and out of doggo's sight.*

10. *If your companion finds the toy you moved, bring out the unscented toy and give it to doggo to play with as a reward.*

11. *Increase the distance and number of boxes you use over time to strengthen this skill and your dog's tracking abilities.*

When playing any of these mentally stimulating games, make sure you're not coaxing doggo and giving away the answers. It is acceptable to provide a small hint or a bit of guidance at first in order for your pooch to understand the ground rules. But this should not become habitual as it will defeat the purpose of the exercises.

These games will not only keep that snout moving and improve the sniffer, but they will also mentally stimulate your canine as well as keep that body moving, contributing to physical health. Again, there are many toys on the market that are great for scent games, such as treat puzzle toys like the Treat Maze interactive puzzle dog toy for instance. Go have a look to see what there is and as suggested, mix the homemade varieties up with some store bought options to keep things interesting and broaden that mutty mind.

CHAPTER 12:
AGILITY GAMES

You've probably seen those hounds that appear to be trained in the manner of a show horse, zipping and zooming around obstacle courses, displaying spectacular skills that appear more precise than a gymnast's motions.

This is known as dog agility, and the good news is that it is not just for pooches competing on professional levels; you can do it in your own capacity with your beloved furry ball. You wouldn't even need any fancy equipment; a simple broom, a couple of buckets, and some boxes would suffice.

Aside from boosting not only physical agility but mental agility as well, this game works wonders for boosting self-confidence, self-control, improved distraction control, and brushing up on those natural instincts. More good news is the fact that when you hone in on the fun with doggo, research has shown that you will be enjoying some fantastic benefits as well (Zoom Room Press. 2023).

Agility training is appropriate for any breed dog, though herding breeds like border collies have a natural instinct to nail it from the start, but this doesn't mean your tiny dog breed can't enjoy the circuit. The one thing you must be mindful of is your hound's physical health; if they have any heart conditions or breathing difficulties, for example, these should be taken into account. Older dogs and dogs with physical health issues should play these games at a much lower intensity and at a much slower pace. Another factor to consider is that your dog needs to understand all of the fundamental cues, such as "sit", "down", and "come", to name a few.

With that said, let us look at some agility games that you and your companion can enjoy.Games

Jump Hurdles

Jumping hurdles, as the name implies, is the act of constructing hurdles for your doggo to jump over. But, before you start pulling out broomsticks and rods, you should know how tall your dog should be in order to set up the appropriate hurdle height. I'm referring to the withers height, which is measured from the highest point of the shoulder blade right down to the floor. Here's a general rule of thumb for the relationship between hurdle and doggo height:

- For dogs with withers that are 11 inches or shorter, a jump height of 4 inches is preferred.

- An 8-inch jump height is suitable for dogs with withers between 11 and 14 inches high.

- For hounds with withers measuring 14 to 18 inches, the jump height is 12 inches.

- For larger companions whose withers measure 18 inches or more, a 16-inch jump height is appropriate.

How To:

Location- this game may be conducted both indoors and outdoors.

1. *You'll need some form of rod; a shovel, shower curtain rod, or the handle of a broomstick would all do. You might also use a pool noodle or a hula hoop as an alternative.*

2. *You may also wrap the pole with a pool noodle for additional safety.*

3. *Use chairs, crates, laundry baskets, or any other items that are the right height for your dog to balance the jumping rod.*

4. *Put duct tape on both pole edges to connect them to the balance items on either side of the pole.*

CHARLOTTE NELSON | 97

5. *Start off slowly and prompt them with a cue of your choosing.*

6. *You will have to repeat this a couple of times and off course seal every jump off with a treat and plenty of praise.*

Weave Poles

Aside from playing catch, this is some real backyard entertainment for doggo, weaving and knotting through upright poles while those muscles and mind get to work.

How To:

Location- this game may be conducted outdoors.

1. *You can use cones, bamboo rods, or some recycled water bottles filled with water.*

2. *Be sure you do not space these too close to each, nothing less than 24 inches apart, other to avoid any collisions or other injuries.*

3. *You have guessed it, lead with a treat in order to show and tell for your fido to understand what it's all about.*

4. *You can gradually increase their speed as they become more familiar with the game.*

Agility Tunnel

Who doesn't love a tunnel? Coming across as this magical abyss, with the added excitement of a treat at the end for your four-footer, this is a simple and enjoyable way for you to instill feelings of success and confidence in your dog.

How To:

Location- this game may be conducted both indoors and outdoors.

1. *Of course, you'll need some sort of tunnel; don't worry, you can easily make one by pushing a few tables together and covering it with a blanket or table cloth, or you can buy an inexpensive kid's play tunnel.*

2. *Simply cue and coax your dog through the tunnel, be sure to have a treat ready on the other side.*

3. *Some furballs may refuse to go all the way to the end of the tunnel. Gently guide them through with patience to instill some confidence.*

The Dog Walk

This is a very simple game, it consists of ramps that lead up to either side of an elevated walkway.

How To:

Location- this game may be conducted both indoors and outdoors.

1. *You'll need to get creative and build this little setup out of a bench and planks on either side to simulate ramps.*

2. *Again, a cue and some guidance will be required to coax doggo up the ramp.*

3. *In order to establish a bit of familiarity, you may need to place them near the end of the walkway and gradually help them down.*

4. *Remember to keep a positive, excited tone of voice to ensure that it is encouraging and establishing a positive association.*

The Teeter Board

The teeter board tends to be a bit more tricky because it involves movement of an object, thus your furry friend needs to be comfortable with this aspect first and foremost.

How To:

Location- this game may be conducted both indoors and outdoors.

1. *You must begin slowly in order to instill confidence in your pet regarding moving objects.*

2. *A skateboard or a toy wagon that is not too high off the ground can be used.*

3. *As you cue them to get onto the object of choice, reward their bravery with a treat.*

4. *They will eventually show interest by putting a paw on it or climbing on top of it on their own.*

5. *Remember that every effort they make should be praised or rewarded in order to reinforce that positive association.*

6. *When your doggo is comfortable on these objects, you can progress to using a plank balanced over a small diameter pipe to keep it low to the ground.*

7. *Cue doggo along the plank while guiding your mutt and providing reinforcement, praise, and security as the plank tips to maintain their confidence.*

8. *With more experience on doggo's side, you can gradually begin using pipes with larger diameters to increase the height.*

It goes without saying, more agile doggos will catch on a lot quicker with these games whereas older or more passive dogs will take a bit longer. If you see you are having some trouble getting the game established, simply try a different approach or game.

CHAPTER 13:
FOCUS GAMES

MENTAL EXERCISE FOR DOGS

CHARLOTTE NELSON

It is critical for your dog to be able to focus, and it all begins with their ability to focus on you.

Doggo must be able to listen to you without being distracted in order to learn tricks, play games, and exercise. Focusing on you is important not only for their behavior, but also for when they need to be soothed and comforted when they are scared or aggressive. Thus, "watch me" should be at the top of your list of cues to teach doggo because it is the key to getting doggo to focus, unlocking all subsequent cues.

Getting any aspect under control, whether it's obedience or behavior issues, begins with your four-foot focusing on you. Let's look at how you can foster this vital aspect.

GAMES

Name Game

Let's start with one of the most crucial focus games before moving on to the others: training your four-footer to focus on you. It is crucial for your doggo to learn that when you say their name, their attention should be on you, eyes and all, without getting sidetracked.

How To:

Location- this game may be conducted both indoors and outdoors.

1. *Choose a location with few distractions, and make sure the snacks are ready and waiting.*

2. *Say your companion's name, then the cue "watch me" or "look," for example.*

3. *If they look at you and you can tell they're paying attention, give them the trusted treat.*

4. *This is unlikely to happen on the first try; therefore on the the second try, you should wait a moment, repeating the "watch me" cue, as you get doggo's attention with a treat and then hold it up to your face to establish recognition.*

5. *Seal it with a treat if doggo gets the idea, as well as a response cue, such as "good job," for extra reinforcement.*

6. *To proof the behavior, increase the distance and change the environments.*

Engage & Disengage

This game is not only great for establishing focus but also works great to brush up on those impulse control skills.

How To:

Location- this game may be conducted both indoors and outdoors.

1. *Pick a cue word such as "yes" and have those treats ready.*

2. *First and foremost, you must establish a link between your chosen que, "Yes," and doggo receiving a treat.*

3. *Simply say the word "Yes" and then give your pet a treat. Voila!*

4. *Repeat this 5 or more times until you can see that an association has been established in which every time the cue is heard, a treat follows.*

5. *The next step will be to engage doggo with this cue.*

6. *Use the cue everytime something is in the vicinity that has a tendency to get your pooch excited, whether it be a person, cyclist, or another dog for example.*

7. *As soon as doggo engages with one of these external factors, such as a person, cyclist, or another dog, give the cue.*

8. *Ascertain that your dog's attention is no longer focused on these variables after the cue.*

9. *If this is successful, give that trusted treat that is associated with the cue.*

10. *Once doggo understands engagement, you can progress by introducing disengagement.*

11. *If a distraction, such as a person, cyclist, or another dog, appears and gets doggo excited, do not cue this time.*

12. *Before cueing, wait a few moments until doggo looks at you first.*

13. *When you get that look back, that's when you use your cue, signifying disengagement, and of course, sealed with a treat.*

Watch Me

This strategy is an excellent addition to the focus game routine, very similar to the name game, however, it only involves establishing eye contact.

How To:

Location- this game may be conducted both indoors and outdoors.

1. *Get doggo to look you in the eyes by using your "Watch me," or any other preferred cue, or by bringing a treat to your nose.*

2. *When those beady eyes lock with yours, reinforce the action with another cue like "Yes," followed by a treat.*

3. *Be mindful of your timing because those little eyes will quickly wander off to the treat, and it is critical to give the enforcement cue when doggo looks into your eyes.*

4. *Repeat this 5 or more times or until the behavior is established.*

5. *After doggo has caught on to this, you can up the stakes by holding a treat in your one hand and placing your finger on your nose as you cue doggo.*

6. *This should be repeatedly done until the behavior is established.*

7. *If your pet locks his or her gaze on you, it is time to reward the behavior.*

8. *The grand finale of the game is to see if doggo looks you in the eyes without being asked.*

9. *If doggo responds, use a reinforcement cue like "Good dog," followed by a treat.*

The Touch Game

This is known as targeting, and the goal is to get you foo-foo to touch your hand with that wet nose. Since it makes life so much simpler when it comes to any cooperative chores or actions, such as teaching a new trick, moving around, and even demonstrating comfort and care during medical treatments, teaching this skill is quite advantageous to nurture.

How To:

Location- this game may be conducted both indoors and outdoors.

1. *Once more, you'll need to start with a cue, so make sure the treats are prepared.*

2. *To scent your hands, you have two options: touch the treats, or hold it in your one hand.*

3. *Stretch your arm out and hold your treat scented hand about 3 inches away from doggo's nose.*

4. *Cue your companion to "Touch".*

5. *It's crucial to offer the reinforcement cue as soon as that wet nose makes physical contact with your palm, followed by rewarding the behavior with a treat.*

6. *Keeping timing in mind, it's key.*

7. *This practice should be repeated a few times before you begin to progressively pull your hand away while holding it at various sides or heights.*

8. *Start over with your prompt cue and follow the customary contact, cue, and reward sequence.*

The important thing is to make these focus games fun for doggo in order to establish a positive association with you, so all of the treats used are to put you in a good light, making you look like an automatic treat dispenser, which of course doggo loves.

This is all to teach your four-legged friend that whenever his or her focus and attention is on you, only good things will happen, thereby encouraging your companion to pay more attention to you, more frequently. I'm sure many human school teachers wished for a method like this.

CHAPTER 14:
IMPULSE CONTROL GAMES

MENTAL EXERCISE FOR DOGS

CHARLOTTE NELSON

You are just as guilty at times for lacking impulse control as your fido is, thus do not assume that it's just a "dog thing".

Consider binge eating, "retail therapy," or endless smartphone scrolling. Guilty? Your dog did not come with a built-in and ready-to-go factory-installed impulse control, and they, like children, must be taught to control their impulses. The earlier one begins, the better.

This is not an overnight process; rather, it is a gradual process that takes place over time, well into your dog's adulthood. As a result, impulse control training and playing these types of games on a regular basis are crucial in the life of any doggo.

If your dog engages in behaviors like jumping up on humans, chasing after other animals, stealing food off the table, or pulling on the leash, to mention a few, you should start including lots of impulse control activities in your daily routine with doggo. As a reason, it's crucial to start by teaching your mutt the fundamentals, such as how to sit and stay. After all, if these conditions are correctly understood and followed on doggo's behalf, there will be no jumping or stealing.

Impulse control games will help reduce frustration and lay the groundwork for a well-trained dog, so let us focus on how you can cultivate this aspect simply by having some good fun with your companion.

GAMES

The SMART x 50 Game

We have SMART goals, but your companion has SMART x 50! All of this sounds great, especially if you are a dog, but what does it mean?

In the same way that the human SMART acronym stands for specific, measurable, achievable, relevant, and time-bound when it comes to achieving goals, SMART x 50 stands for:

- See

- Mark

- And

- Reward

- Training

- And x 50 signifies that doggo will be rewarded a whopping fifty times a day by you.

In this particular instance, I would say that being a canine appears to be the more appealing option. This simple yet powerful game will require you to keep an eye out for any good doggo behaviors throughout the day and act fast. Let's have a look at how this works.

How To:

Location- this game may be conducted both indoors and outdoors.

1. *First thing's first, you are going to have to make sure that you have a sturdy little stash of 50 treats stacked somewhere that is easily accessible.*

2. *Now you just simply go about your usual day, but you need to keep an eye on that pooch of yours, because everytime doggo does something great, such as being obedient or displaying some impressive behavior, you are going to have to promptly reward it.*

3. *This reinforces whatever positive behaviors you are rewarding, and with time your fido will realize that these actions are good, thus naturally performing them more without needing any cues.*

Wait for It

This game is a "winner-winner-chicken-dinner" for you if you frequently question whether you actually fed your dog because the food disappears as soon as you set it down.

Some dogs have a propensity to eat their meals as if it were the last, and in situations like this, it is obvious that exercising some impulse control would be beneficial.

How To:

Location- this game may be conducted both indoors and outdoors.

1. *This game occurs at every meal.*

2. *Hold your four-bowl footer's at about hip height and cue him to wait while you slowly lower the bowl.*

3. *As a reinforcement, reward your doggo with a treat, not the meal, for waiting patiently.*

4. *If your companion comes too close to the bowl, simply cue "No" and lift the bowl.*

5. *Lower the bowl again as you give the wait cue.*

6. *If the bowl is on the floor, reward your doggo with a treat as reinforcement for good behavior.*

7. *This process must be repeated at least five times for it to take root in that little poochy mind.*

8. *But you're not done yet; stage two awaits.*

9. *Allow the bowl to rest on the floor for a few seconds.*

10. *If your canine companion does not approach it, you know what to do: treat time.*

11. *Begin by increasing the waiting times and changing your behavior, such as doing something else instead of standing guard over the bowl.*

12. *Once you've mastered the last step, you can incorporate the release cue.*

13. *Remember that, with the exception of the final step, you must reward good behavior with a treat for every increment of waiting.*

Feeding Hand

This is the "dog world" equivalent of teaching "You can have dessert if you eat all your vegetables," which is based on the Premack Principle.

This principle, in short, is very powerful when it comes to influencing learning because it uses a more desirable behavior or activity, such as eating dessert, to reinforce a less desirable one, such as eating vegetables.

How To:

Location- this game may be conducted both indoors and outdoors.

1. *Surprise, surprise, you will require treats!*

2. *Pop them in one of your hands and cue your furry friend to sit down.*

3. *Keep your hand with the treats closed and lower it to your dog's nose or just above it.*

4. *Of course, your companion will sniff, lick, and possibly nibble on your hand because that snout will sniff all the goodies contained within.*

5. *Ignore it completely. Do not say anything and pay no attention.*

6. *Your fido will eventually become bored and seize the acts of curiosity; this is your cue to slowly open your hand.*

7. *Your companion will return to continue the investigation, if this happens, immediately close your hand.*

8. *Repeat this exercise until doggo loses interest to the extent where there is no approach made to investigate, even if your hand is open.*

9. *It is time to reward him once he has reached the point where he can simply sit still and observe the treats without approaching your hand.*

Stop n' Go

The key to impulse control is delayed gratification, or learning to wait. Something that many of us could do to advance humanity. This simple game is a lot of fun and a fantastic way to practice the "Come" and "Stay" commands while teaching delayed gratification.

How To:

Location- this game may be conducted both indoors and outdoors.

1. *You will only require your beautiful voice and the usual suspects: treats.*

2. *Make some room between yourself and your woofer.*

3. *Cue your fido to come to you.*

4. *However, before your doggo reaches you, call a stop cue.*

5. *Just be patient, and remember to keep calm and watch your tone of voice, because this might take a few strikes before the penny drops.*

6. *Just keep repeating the process, and when your dog succeeds, it's time for another treat.*

7. *Repeat this game a few times to ensure that it sticks.*

Working on impulse control will not only result in a dog with more confidence, self-control, and obedience, but it will also contribute to a closer, calmer bond between you two by encouraging better communication and understanding.

The appeal of all of these games is that they overlap, thus the advantages of each game do not exist in isolation. For instance, the game muffin tin combines a food game with a hunting game, as well as a scent game. To keep your lord or lady of the manor amused and in peak mental and physical condition, mix these games up in your routine.

You will also benefit a great deal from this in terms of the enjoyment you will derive from merely observing how that hairy ball of fuzzy love interacts, responds, and passes the time.

CHAPTER 15:
WATER GAMES

MENTAL EXERCISE FOR DOGS

CHARLOTTE NELSON

Perfect for summer days when it's warm and bright, especially if your doggo is a wet and wild snoot.

Aside from giving such a beautiful sensation of freedom and being a better option than attacking your sprinklers, water activities are fantastic for whole body workouts, including cognitively training that tiny peanut.

This joint-friendly method of exercise and play works wonders for injury recovery by lowering pain and inflammation, and is excellent for dogs with age-related limitations. It is great for weight regulation and cardiovascular conditioning. Water sports provide stimulation that, thanks to the release of all that stored energy, also aids in better regulating stress and sleep.

Let's have a look at some summer day water play options.

GAMES

Dog Dive

With this game, water-loving hounds and retrievers who enjoy getting their ears wet will undoubtedly have a dog house full of fun. It's all about getting sinking toys out of the water.

How To:

Location- this game may be conducted outdoors.

1. *You will need a toy of sorts with a bit of weight that will allow it to sink slowly to the bottom.*

2. *Start off in shallow water in order for doggo to understand how the game works.*

3. *Cue your doggo to sit before you simply toss the toy into the water.*

4. *Cue doggo to dive in and retrieve.*

5. *Call your mutt, and of course, praise and a treat are part of the deal.*

6. *Start slowly and gradually increase the toss distance as your dog becomes more comfortable with the game.*

Flirt Pole Fishing

You can also play fetch in the water, but if your four-footer isn't into fetch, you can use a flirt pole, which is essentially a long stick with a rope at one end and a toy attached to it, similar to a fishing rod. However, flirt pole fun is not limited to the water; it can also be enjoyed on land.

How To:

Location- this game may be conducted both indoors and outdoors.

1. *You obviously need a flirt pole; you can either buy one or get creative and make one yourself, as with most toys in these activities.*

2. *Cue your companion to sit, and simply drop the flirt pole's toy end into the water.*

3. *Now you can cue for fetching or fishing by tugging, dipping, and pulling the toy through the water for doggo to catch.*

4. *Just be careful not to get carried away; you'll need to let doggo make the catch of the day to keep your mutt from becoming frustrated or bored with the game.*

5. *When the "fish" has been caught, seal the deal with some praise and a treat.*

6. *This game could be enjoyed indoors as well by utilizing a bucket or even the bathtub, just be sure to make provision for a lot of splashing. Hence if you are in the mood to taste some soap, this might serve as a great opportunity for some bath time as well.*

Floating

If your woofer isn't particularly fond of getting wet, that doesn't mean they should avoid water games entirely. You have options, and they are quite exciting, as many a dog can attest. I'm referring to boat rides, paddle boards, and surf boards.

How To:

Location- this game may be conducted outdoors.

1. *You will need any of the above mentioned, even a pool lilo or any other floating alternative that can sustain your woofer's weight.*

2. *Start off slowly yet again, you will have to provide some extra support and comfort as this is a moving object and might come across as rather intimidating for your doggo at first.*

3. *You can cue them to either sit or stand as you hold and guide them a short distance floating across the water.*

4. *Continue making short trips initially until familiarity is established.*

5. *You can increase the trip distance as well as your distance from them if you see their confidence is sufficient and they have mastered the balancing act required by this game.*

6. *To ensure water safety, keep an eye on them while they are floating around, as they may become tired or frustrated and jump into the water.*

Sprinklers and Splash Pools

Location- this game may be conducted outdoors.

Sprinklers are a magnet for some dogs, so take advantage of this fact and incorporate it into your agility game obstacle course. This will be ideal as a grand finale to run through and cool down at the end of the course. Look into sprinkler pads which are essentially interactive playgrounds spouting little fountains of water that doggo can play and run through.

If you don't have a pool in your backyard or another body of water nearby, a baby pool will suffice when it comes to cooling down your doggo. You can fill it with floating toys, perhaps even a scented chew toy, to give your four-footer a little extra hunting fun.

Doggo can transform into a hairy water mermaid with games like fetch, frisbee, catch, or tag for instance, that can all be played in water as well.

Before diving in and making a splash, it's critical to understand water safety for your four-footer.

WATER SAFETY

Let us look at some water safety pointers that you should take to heart.

Take It Slow

Getting your pooch used to water is a process in all honesty, whether they love water or not. It is all about instilling the right behaviors in order to make sure this fun is enjoyed safely. If your doggo is new to water games, start off shallow and slow. You'll want to monitor their behavior to make sure that it is something they will truly end up enjoying, rather than something that brings forth any sense of anxiety.

Not All Doggos Love Water

You are more than welcome to test the waters to see if your woofer is interested, but never force the issue. Be especially cautious if your dog has a short snoot, as in the case of Chihuahuas, because any water inhaled through those muzzles can result in pneumonia.

Invest in a Life Vest

Life vests are fantastic for water safety, especially when the water level is higher than your companion's head. Most come with a leash attachment, which is useful in emergency situations such as when your dog jumps out of a boat for instance. This is also great for keeping them afloat, providing that extra bit of safety if they get tired.

Supervision

As with children, your water woofer must at all times be supervised when they are splashing about in any pool of water. Unfortunate accidents do happen, thus it is best to be aware in order to prevent or be able to immediately respond with regards to anything going wrong.

Just be sure to always have fresh water at hand, because any water game is physically exertive and can bring about colossal bouts of thirst. With this being said, recreational water is not the same as drinking water. Be sure doggo does not drink any water from the pool, lake, sea, or dam. Pool chemicals are evidently not fit for consumption and you never know what might be floating around in a given body of water.

At the end of the day, going for a simple swim also has its benefits, and what better way to bond with doggo than getting fit together, swimming off into the horizon of whichever body of water you find yourselves in.

CHAPTER 16:
MENTAL HEALTH

MENTAL EXERCISE FOR DOGS

CHARLOTTE NELSON

You can never argue the undevoted love and loyalty your companion has for you, hence considered man's best friend. Nothing makes that fur ball happier than you, well, maybe the occasional treat, but we can safely say it's you.

Making certain that this is reciprocated in the relationship is critical; after all, isn't that what relationships are all about, giving and receiving? You can cultivate the emotional, physical, and mental support your beloved companion requires with these exercises and information. But let us take it a step further by expanding on what you know and take a closer look at the mental aspect for a moment.

I say this because, like humans, dogs have complex mental processes and can also suffer from depression, anxiety, and other similar issues. The big difference is that we can talk about how we feel and what we are experiencing, whereas your doggo cannot. This emphasizes the importance of knowing the ins and outs of what to look for in terms of your mutt's mental health.

COMMON CONDITIONS

Let's examine some of the most prevalent mental health problems that dogs have. As you'll see, they are all the same as those that people experience.

This is not something to be taken lightly since the anguish that such a devoted, compassionate little heart will have to face will be horrifying. Knowing how horrible it is and how it impacts our lives, you only need to be aware that it is no different when it comes to a canine, thus cultivating awareness with regards to these issues forms a cornerstone of responsible pet parenting.

Obsessive Compulsive Disorder

No, it's not just humans who obsessively repeat behaviors; your dog can too, and as you know, obsessive compulsive disorder, or OCD, can be quite frustrating, debilitating, and when it comes to canines, dangerous as well.

Canine compulsive disorder develops when routine habits such as engaging with you or eating become excessive; the behavior can sometimes become so out of control that it causes injury. Unfortunately, some breeds are more prone to this condition than others, including Dobermans, Great Danes, and Border Collies to name a few. Thus, a little extra research will go a long way in determining if your dog is prone to this disorder by looking at all dog breeds that fall into this category.

- Be on the lookout for signs which include:
- Tail or shadow chasing
- Incessant licking
- Biting at invisible objects
- Spinning
- Pacing

Many of these behaviors do occur in dogs, but pay attention to how frequently they occur and be sure to regulate your doggo's behavior before and after these instances to look for any other signs of distress.

Depression

You don't have to be a rocket scientist to figure out why your dog is depressed; because dogs are such emotional creatures, they fall into depression for many of the same reasons we do.

Generally caused by environmental factors, the following are examples:

- Bereavement, whether human or animal.

- When their needs are not met, they experience a sense of neglect.

- Adapting to a change in routine or location.

- Any causes or symptoms of pain or discomfort.

When your dog appears withdrawn, struggles to eat, exhibits signs of lethargy, and plays much less, you should conduct further investigation to determine whether these symptoms are indicative of a deeper issue that needs to be addressed.

Anxiety

Anxiety in your dog denotes a constant state of stress as well as being hypervigilant the majority of the time.

Look out for any of the following indicators:

- Easily triggered.

- Inability to decompress and relax.

- Being alone causes a great deal of distress.

- Reacting negatively to stimuli such as people, noises, or animals.

With people going back to work and life getting back to normal, separation anxiety has been on the rise, especially post-Covid, uprooting that sense of comfort and creating a great deal of distress for furry friends.

Separation anxiety indicators include:

- Escape attempts.

- Relieving themselves in the house even if they are housetrained.

- Excessive pacing.

- Destructive behaviors such as chewing.

Anxiety in dogs is typically treated through supplementation, behavioral modification, or medication, depending on the severity and how they respond to various types of treatment.

Post-Traumatic Stress Disorder

As with people, dogs who experience any kind of abuse, trauma, or neglect can acquire post-traumatic stress disorder, or PTSD. This is especially highly prevalent in K9s and retired military dogs as well.

As you are aware, neglect and abuse alone are a serious concern in terms of animal rights violations and inflict tremendous trauma. Getting expert therapy is strongly advised when it comes to PTSD because it has a cluster of symptoms from different other mental health illnesses. They, like us, have the right to feel safe, loved, and cared for and also deserve to live a fulfilled life. Thus getting professional help is highly recommended when it comes to PTSD because it has a cluster of symptoms from various other mental health disorders.

Aside from knowing your dog's history, including whether or not they have been neglected, abused, or subjected to other forms of trauma, the following could be signs of PTSD:

- Chronic anxiety

- Hypervigilance

- Overly sensitive to noises

- Aggression

- Sleeping difficulties

- Hiding or escaping

Unfortunately, this condition is not easily cured; thus, PTSD necessitates the assistance of a qualified veterinarian and is frequently treated with medication and behavioral therapy. To aid in any form of healing, pets suffering from PTSD should be placed in trigger-free environments that instill calm and a sense of security.

Dementia

Dementia in dogs is known as canine cognitive dysfunction, or CCD, and is unfortunately quite common among four-footers.

Though these symptoms, such as memory, learning, and comprehension decline, are treatable, there is no cure for this disease. The only thing you can do is provide appropriate medication and supplementation, as well as keep an eye on that diet because it can help slow the progression of dementia.

Dementia is difficult to diagnose, so it is diagnosed by a vet through a process of elimination. The following are some signs to look for and discuss with your veterinarian to alert them to the possibility of dementia in your companion:

- Inability to recognize familiar objects, places, or people.

- Memory loss, forgetting behaviors and commands, and failing to respond when called

- Restlessness or aversion to movement can both develop into general behaviors

- Being disoriented and withdrawing

- Going to the bathroom in the house, irrespective of being housetrained

When your doggo is diagnosed with dementia, the only thing you can do is provide extra tender love and care, as well as ensure that all medications and supplements are taken to ensure the best end-of-life care possible.

MANAGING MENTAL HEALTH DISORDERS

Some conditions can be cured over time, while others must be managed on an ongoing basis, depending on the severity of the condition and how your mutt responds to various treatments.

A healthy, fulfilled life is, however, possible with the proper diagnosis and care. As a result, professional diagnoses and guidance are highly recommended, allowing you to take the appropriate action and provide much-needed support.

Let's examine some actions you can take when your dog receives a mental health issue diagnosis:

A Change of Environment

Paying attention to the surroundings at home will be one of the first things you must do. Watch out for anything in your personal space that can trigger something that makes them more prone to feeling or magnifying any types of distress.

It could be necessary to replace some toys with calming alternatives, restrict exposure to strangers, or cut back on trips to parks where they might become overstimulated. This will make it easier to manage these problems because it will help prevent or decrease the reactive state that many of these disorders cause.

Identify Triggers

Speaking of avoiding stressors and eliminating exposure to triggers, you will have to be able to identify what triggers your companion. The most common stressors for doggos include children, new surroundings, strangers, loud noises, and other pets for instance.

Routine Is Key

A sense of familiarity, security, and safety can be built through routine. So make sure you arrange and adhere to every mealtime, playtime, and bathroom break. If there are any new modifications that need to be made to the timetable, be sure to do so gradually to prevent any additional stress.

Avoid Reinforcement of Negative Behaviors

A number of these circumstances can test your patience, so be patient when handling them. It's crucial to always maintain your composure and remain calm. No shouting overly consoling your doggo when a distressing behavior pops up. To the extent feasible, maintain your neutrality to prevent promoting this negative behavior that stems from distress.

Limit Alone Time

Canines of all breeds are pack animals, so if they could talk, they would tell you that they adore you, enjoy treats, and dislike being alone.

Companionship is an instinctive part of their survival instinct. As a result, leaving them alone for extended periods of time has a negative impact on their mental health. If you know you'll be working extra hours or going on vacation, it's best to find a pet sitter, whether it's a friend, family member, or a dog hotel, if they won't be able to accompany you.

Regular Vet Visits

Keeping up with your dog's health is essential for maintaining peak physical and mental wellbeing, so regular vet visits are required to best monitor these aspects. After all, if you are required to go for regular check ups with your health care practitioner to keep you informed and up to date with regard to your health, same goes for doggo with a pumping heart and a treat breath.

You can even look into getting pet insurance to aid with medical costs.

Regular Exercise

And this is why I wanted to focus on these mental exercises in the book; they are both physically and mentally engaging, and necessitate interaction from your side, all of which contribute to your companion living a happy and fulfilled life.

You'd think this would be self-evident, but many people overlook this basic fact. Thinking that if doggo is fed and has plenty of space to run around in, that's all that's required. Nothing could be further from the truth. They need to be exposed to new places and experiences, and aside from physical activity, they need your interaction to form bonds and foster their mental health. Thus, regular physical exercise is more than just running around; it is about keeping both the mind and the body fit and healthy. After all, these two aspects are extremely dependent on each other when it comes to living a well-balanced life, as one cannot exist without the other.

Just as your mental health is important, so are your furry companions, and just as your mental health requires daily attention, so do your furry companions. Their health and longevity are dependent on being in peak physical and mental condition, so take these guidelines to heart and follow them routinely to ensure the best for your fido.

CONCLUSION

MENTAL EXERCISE FOR DOGS

CHARLOTTE NELSON

And now we have reached the end of your lovely voyage of little tips, tricks, and all things you can get right with treats, when it comes to keeping your beloved furry addition to your family healthy, happy, and cognitively sharp.

Now, in your life there will be very little you will come across that would ever appreciate the sheer genius of your conversation the way your beloved companion does. Aside from the fact that it does not imply that you are a genius, the very special bond that forms between man or woman and their best friend is something that is truly irreplaceable.

Always ready to comfort, lean in with a lick, or open to a hug and a cuddle, the non-judgement and loyalty provided by four-footed fur balls has been proven to hold so many benefits for us as humans. Some of the best therapists are indeed furry and four-legged. Thus, don't think you're the only one doing favors, because there's nothing better than someone who will just listen to you at times—someone with whom you can be silly and let go of the reality of the big world filled with responsibilities.

Doggos aren't just about filling the empty space on the couch, keeping the kids happy, filling a void in your life, or fitting in with the rest of society. They are far more important than that. Canines are a true source of happiness, and tell you what, there is only one other that has the same unconditional love for you as your mother does, and that is your canine. Coming to think of it, who else could you tell a secret and be assured that it will never be repeated?

And, if you want to amplify all these benefits and emotions, which is entirely possible, you should undoubtedly spend that extra time with your woofer and put in some training, exercise, and mental games. The results?

A better understanding of each other, which leads to more enjoyable times, increased trust, and a stronger bond. For your doggo, this means a sense of self-confidence, independence, and better impulse control, among a laundry list of other benefits.

And how can you tell if your doggo is reaching that milestone of being properly trained?

Well, you can tell if your doggo is well-trained when there are no longer attempts to steal your dinner or lunch, but rather the guilt bestowed upon you by one glance of those beady little eyes which will force you to share.

In this book you have gained a better understanding of the importance of physical activity and mental stimulation for your four-footer. Personally, one of the most important reasons I appreciate my companion's physical and mental well-being is that it increases life expectancy. And you have to admit, having hair covered clothing is not something that will ever deter you from not wanting that mutt around for a very, very long time.

You have also had a look into how to understand your pooch better with regards to their body language, essentially speaking "dog". Hopefully, you will become more fluent with this new information, allowing you to not only better understand your doggo, but also meet his or her needs and gauge his or her emotions. It is critical for you to interpret your lord or lady of the manor's nonverbal body language in order to determine whether they are happy, distressed, or in need of something.

In short, you can better care for your furry buddy if you understand how they communicate with you through their various tail positions, such as the loose wag, low-hung, and high-stiff, cues, postures, and beady eyes. We all understand how crucial effective communication is in any relationship, and this factor plays a significant role in any given relationship.

We discussed different toys, the value of diversity and size, as well as the significance of taking your mutt's age and personality into account. In order to supplement doggo's collection, we also looked into a variety of other toy categories that are available out there.

Before entering all of the games, knowledge of training advice laid the foundation. Here, we examined issues including avoiding interruptions, developing patience, and the significance of repetition and consistency in order to reinforce certain behaviors. Another noteworthy aspect of this situation is how crucial timing those snacks is to the entire procedure.

Never underestimate your critter's intelligence; you think that fur ball can't count? Try holding four treats in your hand and only giving your fido two; as a result, those sharp minds are watching you closely, and your timing has to be perfect—even better than when you do the tango. If you time it incorrectly, you may instill the wrong behavior.

We focused on training and examined the science behind various methods based on operant conditioning, which is based on the principle of adding or subtracting something. Looking at the four quadrants of operant conditioning, we determined that positive reinforcement combined with negative punishment are the best options to use when training that foo-foo of yours. Positive reinforcement is preferred because it is more humane and compassionate, and it is critical for maintaining established trust as well as the "learning is fun" aspect.

We moved on to some training mistakes that you should avoid in the same way that you would avoid stepping in a pile of poop. These included, among other things, futile repetition, cue poisoning, one trick at a time, and knowing when enough is enough. And, since we've established that nagging exists in the "dog world," keep an eye on how you communicate with your four-footer.

Following that, the subject of children, dogs, and visits was raised, with the primary concern being the safety of all parties involved. It was discussed how to prepare your doggo for visitors while also establishing boundaries and rules. Getting your pooch used to children entails exposing your mutt to children, whether through a park, exposure to children's toys, or even you letting loose and acting like a child yourself, all of which were factors we considered to ensure smooth social sailing. But it wasn't just about your doggo; it was also about communicating to the kids what is and isn't allowed. How to introduce them to doggo, what is permitted with doggo, and when to avoid your mutt, no matter how cuddly and irresistibly fuzzy your four-footer is.

Let the games begin with all of the information and examples of mentally stimulating games you can play with your furry friend. These are just a few basic examples to help you understand what it's all about. As previously stated, many of these games serve dual purposes; for example, some are good for honing those sniffing senses as well as hunting or agility. At the end of the day, what matters most is that you try them all out and see which ones your doggo prefers. They, like you, should have fun while learning.

When you play these games with your fido, there will almost certainly be a lot of laughter. Consider the worst-case scenario: your fido does not resonate, and you move on to the next game on the list. The best case scenario is when you can see your doggo catching on and enjoying it, radiating joy, knowledge, and good behavior from that furry body. Just remember these companions are equivalent to having kids, only with extra legs and a whole lot of body hair, thus that time spent together is placed on such high regard with these critters, perhaps even more precious than it is for you.

After all of the fun and games, we had to return to being responsible and investigate a very serious issue concerning your beloved companion; mental health. This was not done to disrupt the party in any way, but rather to arm you with more important information that will allow you to better foster good mental health in your furry friend.

These are serious matters, as serious as it gets when it comes to humans. The significance of spreading knowledge regarding animals' mental health cannot be overstated. People's mental health is receiving a flood of attention, which is one of the best things that has ever existed. However, bear in mind that your canine buddy also benefits from it, making it equally crucial.

You do not have to be a prominent member in society in order for you to properly love, care, and look after your companion. I have seen folks who have much less than others, but those mutts seemed as content as they possibly could. Why? Because, regardless of whether you go out and buy the most hydro mechanical or dyrodynamical toys (you can still make your own at home), what matters is the time, love, care, and compassion you demonstrate. What do you get in exchange? Oh, it's reciprocal; you get the same benefits, but with an added bonus. You receive something extremely rare, more valuable than the most expensive diamond, and this is known as loyalty. Another aspect to consider is that according to some folks, apparently the average dog is nicer than the average person, because making mistakes is part of human nature, but forgiveness is canine. Loyalty, forgiveness, unconditional love? Wow!

In reality, your dog is more than a companion; he is a member of the family. Whether you are married, single, or have nine children, your canine is a part of the weave that makes up the fabric of your life. Four-footers aren't just accessories or fun toys. Thus, after digesting all of this new information, I would like you to take a different stance and see that critter beyond all of that fur: the best listener you could have. Aside from all of this, the physical benefits you will gain from playing and training your beloved companion are far superior to anything you could ever get out of a gym membership. Sure, you don't have any weights or fancy equipment to measure your heart rate or the number of calories you burn, but you do have something far more valuable than any device can produce: content and true friendship.

It's not always easy, that is the truth, but one thing that remains is that what you put in is what you get out, and this is just all based on the true beauty of their innocent nature.

So here are my final words: yes, you can buy happiness, you can buy a dog. But proceed with caution, as doing so could lead to an addiction akin to that of potato chips; you can't just have one, but having a home filled with love and dog hair is better than a somber heart at the end of the day.

I'll say it again: your heart will be stolen, or is already stolen, depending on your current situation. But, at least you won't have to pick up food off the floor if you have this waggy-tailed, furry creature sharing your space.

GLOSSARY

MENTAL EXERCISE FOR DOGS

CHARLOTTE NELSON

Arthritis: a common condition that causes pain and inflammation in a joint.

Associative learning: a learning process in which a new response becomes associated with a particular stimulus.

Cardiovascular health: the health of the heart and blood vessels.

Chronic anxiety: persistent worrying or anxiety about a number of areas that are out of proportion to the impact of the events.

Classical conditioning: learning that happens unconsciously.

Cognitive decline: the experience of worsening or more frequent confusion or memory loss.

Cue: a thing said or done that serves as a signal to perform a certain behavior.

Cue nagging: when owners repeat an instruction or command, such as 'down', 'sit' or 'roll over', over and over, even though their dog isn't listening.

Hypervigilance: the elevated state of constantly assessing potential threats around you

Insulin health: sufficiently enabling your body to turn food into energy and controls your blood sugar levels.

Negative punishment: removal of a pleasant stimulus in order to decrease or discourage a certain behavior.

Negative reinforcement: something unpleasant is removed or taken away to increase the likelihood of a desired behavior.

OCD: obsessive compulsive disorder (OCD) is a common mental health condition where a person has obsessive thoughts and compulsive behaviors.

Operant conditioning: a method of learning that uses reward and punishment to modify specific behaviors.

Positive punishment: introducing a consequence to an unpleasant or unwanted behavior.

Positive reinforcement: introducing a desirable or pleasant stimuli after the performance of a desired behavior.

PTSD: Post-traumatic stress disorder (PTSD) is a mental health problem you may develop after experiencing traumatic event

REFERENCES

MENTAL EXERCISE FOR DOGS

CHARLOTTE NELSON

admin. (n.d.). *30 Dog Games to Play with Pups Young and Old, Indoors and Out*. Https://Www. houndslounge.com/. Retrieved January 4, 2023, from https://www.houndslounge. com/blog/30-dog-games-to-play-with-pups/amp/

Ambler, J., & Demir, N. (2023). *Canine dementia: spotting the signs of dementia in dogs*. Myfamilyvets. https://www.myfamilyvets.co.uk/signs-of-dementia-in-dogs

Association, D. T. (2020, June 5). *Top 10 brain games for your dog with food*. DogTalentAssociation. https://www.dogtalentassociation.com/post/top-10-brain-games-for-your-dog-with-food

August 20, K. V., & 2021. (2021, August 20). *Dog Agility Training Is the Ultimate Boredom Buster*. Daily Paws. https://www.dailypaws.com/dogs-puppies/dog-training/agility-competitive/dog-agility-training

BENDER, A. (2019, September 26). *How to Train Your Dog to Focus on You*. The Spruce Pets. https://www.thesprucepets.com/train-dog-to-look-at-you-1117297

Bender, A. (2022, February 28). *How to Train Your Dog to Be Kid Friendly*. The Spruce Pets. https://www.thesprucepets.com/tips-for-childproofing-a-dog-1117491

BYRNES, C. A. (2018). *How to Play With Your Dog*. Diamondsintheruff. https://www. diamondsintheruff.com/how-to-play

Cavaleri, F., & BSc. (2014, April 29). *The importance of exercise for dogs*. Animal Wellness Magazine. https://animalwellnessmagazine.com/importance-of-exercise-dog/

Day, J. (2022, September 6). *Signs It's Time to End a Training Session*. Www.akcpetinsurance. com. https://www.akcpetinsurance.com/blog/canine-fatigue-6-signs-your-training-session-is-done-

Dog Body Language 101: Understanding Dog Communication. (2022). Www.k9ofmine.com. https://www.k9ofmine.com/dog-body-language/

Dogster. (2012, September 25). *How to Help Hunting Dogs Enjoy a Life Without Hunting*. Dogster. https://www.dogster.com/lifestyle/dog-training-hunting-dogs-life-without

ERIN JONES. (2020, June 26). *8 Dog Training Games to Teach Essential Skills!* Www.k9ofmine. com. https://www.k9ofmine.com/dog-training-games/

facebook/petablecare. (2020, October 26). *7 Benefits of Agility Training for You and Your Dog*. Petable. https://petable.care/2020/10/26/7-benefits-agility-training-dog/

Farricelli, A. (2022, July 31). *10 Impulse Control Games for Dogs*. PetHelpful. https://pethelpful. com/dogs/Impulse-Control-Games-for-Dogs

Ferrer, A. A. (2022, May 27). *Everything to Know About Your Pet's Mental Health.* Money. https://money.com/pet-mental-health/

FRATT, K. (2017, December 21). *22 Best Games to Play With Your Dog: From Learning to Sports!* K9 of Mine. https://www.k9ofmine.com/best-games-to-play-with-dog/

Gibeault, S. (2020, January 27). *Understanding dog body language: Decipher dogs' signs & signals.* American Kennel Club. https://www.akc.org/expert-advice/advice/how-to-read-dog-body-language/

Gibeault, S., MSc, Jun 16, C., Jun 16, 2021 | 4 M., & Minutes, 2021 | 4. (2021, June 16). *Positive Reinforcement Dog Training: The Science Behind Operant Conditioning.* American Kennel Club. https://www.akc.org/expert-advice/training/operant-conditioning-the-science-behind-positive-reinforcement-dog-training/#:~:text=Focus%20on%20Positive%20Reinforcement&text=That%20means%20they%20deal%20with

Hansen Wheat, C., & Temrin, H. (2020). Intrinsic Ball Retrieving in Wolf Puppies Suggests Standing Ancestral Variation for Human-Directed Play Behavior. *IScience*, *23*(2), 100811. https://doi.org/10.1016/j.isci.2019.100811

How to Create a DIY Agility Course in Your Backyard. (2020, April 21). NutriSource Pet Foods. https://nutrisourcepetfoods.com/blog/pet-parents/how-to-create-a-diy-agility-course-in-your-backyard/

How to get your dog's focus and attention | Dogs Trust. (2022). Www.dogstrust.org.uk. https://www.dogstrust.org.uk/dog-advice/training/basics/focus-training

How to Play Safely with Your Dog. (2022). Www.orvis.com. https://www.orvis.com/how-to-play-safely-with-your-dog.html

How to Train Your Dog & Top Training Tips | RSPCA. (2022). Www.rspca.org.uk. https://www.rspca.org.uk/adviceandwelfare/pets/dogs/training

Huntingford, D. J. (2018, June 29). *Why a Dog's Mental Exercise is Just as Important as Physical Exercise.* Blog.petwellbeing.com. https://blog.petwellbeing.com/why-mental-exercise-is-as-important-as-physical-exercise-for-your-dog

Interactive Food Toys. (2022, July 8). American Humane. https://www.americanhumane.org/fact-sheet/interactive-food-toys/

Jan 26, H. E., Jan 26, 2017 | 3 M., & Minutes, 2017 | 3. (2017, January 26). *Dog Training Tips: How to Train a Dog.* American Kennel Club. https://www.akc.org/expert-advice/training/12-useful-dog-training-tips/

Jenkins, E. K., DeChant, M. T., & Perry, E. B. (2018). When the Nose Doesn't Know: Canine Olfactory Function Associated With Health, Management, and Potential Links to Microbiota. *Frontiers in Veterinary Science*, *5*(56). https://doi.org/10.3389/fvets.2018.00056

Johnston, D. (2020, May 26). *How do I get my dog to pay attention to me? Focus Games & Cues!* Https://Dogsdayoutseattle.com/. https://dogsdayoutseattle.com/get-dog-pay-attention-play-focus-games-cues/

Jones, E. (2019, November 22). *Impulse Control Games for Dogs: Teaching Self-Control!* K9 of Mine; K9 of Mine. https://www.k9ofmine.com/impulse-control-games-for-dogs/

Keep Your Dog's Brain Active with Brain Games & Food Puzzles. (n.d.). Www.justrightpetfood. com. Retrieved January 4, 2023, from https://www.justrightpetfood.com/blog/brain-games-for-dogs

Larson, J. (2018, June 20). *70+ Funny Dog Quotes and Sayings.* My Dog's Name. https://www.mydogsname.com/funny-dog-quotes/

Lipman, A. (2022, June 30). *10 Dog Training Tips for First Time Pet Owners.* Blog.homesalive. ca. https://blog.homesalive.ca/dog-blog/dog-training-tips

Lotz, K. (2014, November 19). *How to Cope with Visiting Children & Your Dog.* IHeartDogs. com. https://iheartdogs.com/how-to-cope-with-visiting-children-your-dog/

Lotz, K. (2022, April 7). *5 Common Dog Training Mistakes to Avoid.* American Kennel Club; American Kennel Club. https://www.akc.org/expert-advice/training/train-dog-common-mistakes-avoid%e2%80%8b/

Pratt, J. (2021, October 29). *5 Must Know Tips to Maintain Your Dog's Mental Health.* Walkin' Pets Blog. https://www.handicappedpets.com/blog/maintain-dog-mental-health/

Press, a number of publications D. G. quotes have been published on the A., Creations, H., Petcentric, Pet 360, Financial, O., Company, B., MainStreet, Care.com, & More, M. (2021, October 15). *The Importance of Playing with Your Dog | Sunset Veterinary Clinic.* Www. sunsetvetclinic.com. https://www.sunsetvetclinic.com/the-importance-of-playing-with-your-dog/

Quaranta, A., Siniscalchi, M., & Vallortigara, G. (2007). Asymmetric tail-wagging responses by dogs to different emotive stimuli. *Current Biology*, *17*(6), R199–R201. https://doi.org/10.1016/j.cub.2007.02.008

Rigley, C. (2018). *How to Find Non-Toxic Dog Toys and Tell If a Toy is Safe.* Preventivevet.com. https://www.preventivevet.com/dogs/how-to-find-safe-non-toxic-dog-toys

ROBERTSON, C. (2020, October 6). *7 Nosework Games for Dogs: Stimulate Your Dog Through Scentwork!* Www.k9ofmine.com. https://www.k9ofmine.com/nosework-games-for-dogs/

Ropp, M. (2020, January 11). *30 Funny Dog Quotes Every Dog Lover Will Relate To.* The Dog People by Rover.com. https://www.rover.com/blog/funny-dog-quotes-every-dog-lover-will-relate-to/

Safakish, J. (2020, November 21). *Mental Stimulation For Dogs: Why It's Important & Best Activities Explained.* HolistaPet. https://www.holistapet.com/dog-care/mental-stimulation/

Schipper, L. L., Vinke, C. M., Schilder, M. B. H., & Spruijt, B. M. (2008). The effect of feeding enrichment toys on the behaviour of kennelled dogs (Canis familiaris). *Applied Animal Behaviour Science, 114*(1-2), 182–195. https://doi.org/10.1016/j.applanim.2008.01.001

7 homemade games that stimulate your dog mentally | Non-stop dogwear®. (n.d.). Www.nonstopdogwear.com. Retrieved January 4, 2023, from https://www.nonstopdogwear.com/en/magazine/7-diy-dog-games/

Shastri, A. (2022, November 1). *The Best Cheap Dog Toys: Our Top Picks Reviewed.* Veterinarians.org. https://www.veterinarians.org/cheap-dog-toys/

Shaw, J. (2022, September 21). *How Can I Prepare My Dogs to Visit with Kids?* Vetstreet. https://www.vetstreet.com/our-pet-experts/how-can-i-prepare-my-dogs-to-visit-with-kids

Small Door's medical experts. (2023). *How to Teach Your Dog Agility.* Small Door Veterinary. https://www.smalldoorvet.com/learning-center/behavior/how-to-teach-your-dog-agility

Smirnova, V. (2020, August 28). *Beyond the Doggy Paddle: 10 Fun Water Games to Play with Your Dog - The Dogington Post.* Www.dogingtonpost.com. https://www.dogingtonpost.com/beyond-the-doggy-paddle-10-fun-water-games-to-play-with-your-dog/

Son, K. (2021, August 23). *The Best 12 Interactive Dog Toys to Keep Your Canine Busy.* Veterinarians.org. https://www.veterinarians.org/interactive-dog-toys/

Src='https://Secure.gravatar.com/Avatar/73aa055ccfbfa36b0e3195a27136cd84?s=60, img A., #038;d=mm, Srcset='https://Secure.gravatar.com/Avatar/73aa055c-cfbfa36b0e3195a27136cd84?s=120, 038;r=g', #038;d=mm, & Gait, 038;r=g 2x' class='avatar avatar-60 photo' height='60' width='60' loading='lazy'/>Cathy. (2022, July 6). *The Nose Knows: Nose Work Games for Dogs.* Furtropolis. https://outwardhound.com/furtropolis/dogs/nose-work-games-for-dogs

Team, Y. (2022, June 8). *Importance Of Regular Exercise For Dogs*. Yuvaap - #FindYourY. https://www.yuvaap.com/blogs/importance-of-regular-exercise-for-dogs/

The Benefits Of Rope Toys For Your Dog. (2021, February 18). Multipet. https://www.multipet.com/the-benefits-of-rope-toys-for-your-dog/

The Benefits of Swimming for Dogs. (2020, August 13). Impact Dog Crates. https://www.impactdogcrates.com/blogs/puppy-news/the-benefits-of-swimming-for-dogs#:~:text=Therapeutic%20swimming%20strengthens%20your%20dog

TLC. (2021, October 8). *Why Is Exercise So Important For Dogs? | Wuffes*. Wuffes.com. https://wuffes.com/blogs/news/why-exercise-important-dogs

Top Activities For A Tracking And Hunting Dog - Wag! (2023). WagWalking. https://wagwalking.com/activity/activities-for-a-tracking-and-hunting-dog

Top Activities For Dogs Who Like To Hunt - Wag! (2023). WagWalking. https://wagwalking.com/activity/activities-for-dogs-who-like-to-hunt

21 Common Dog Training Mistakes and How to Fix Them [updated for 2022] | Pupford. (2022, January 25). Pupford.com. https://pupford.com/21-common-dog-training-mistakes/

WebMD Editorial Contributors. (n.d.). *Mental and Physical Activities for Dogs*. WebMD. https://pets.webmd.com/dogs/enriching-your-dogs-life

Why Dogs Need Exercise Importance & Benefits. (2018, May 30). Jet Pet Resort. https://jetpetresort.com/blog/dog-care/the-importance-of-exercising-your-dog/

Writer, T. (2019, August 19). *22 Common Dog Training Mistakes(& Why You Need To Stop Them NOW)*. Dog Sense New Zealand. https://dogsense.co.nz/dog-training-mistakes/

Zoo, T. D. (2021, January 16). *5 Best Mind Stimulating Toys for Dogs- Keep Your Fido Entertained*. Two Dog Zoo. https://twodogzoo.com/best-mind-stimulating-toys-dogs/#:~:text=Best%20Mind%20Stimulating%20Toys%20for%20Dogs%20%20%E2%80%93%20Reviews

Zoom Room Press. (2023). *Dog Agility Research | Exercise Study | Health Benefits*. Zoom Room Dog Training. https://zoomroom.com/pr/dog-agility-exercise-study/

Printed in Great Britain
by Amazon

22543427R00086